MOUNTAIN MAN

01 02 03 04 05 23 22 21 20 19

Caitlin Press Inc
8100 Alderwood Road,
Halfmoon Bay, BC V0N 1Y1
www.caitlin-press.com

Cover design by Vici Johnstone
Text design by Gerilee McBride Design

Printed in Canada

Caitlin Press Inc. acknowledges financial support from the Government of Canada and the Canada Council for the Arts, and the Province of British Columbia through the British Columbia Arts Council and the Book Publisher's Tax Credit.

Canada Council for the Arts | Conseil des Arts du Canada | British Columbia Arts Council | Funded by the Government of Canada | Canada

Library and Archives Canada Cataloguing in Publication

Title: Mountain man : the life of a guide outfitter / by Hiram Cody Tegart and Andrew Bruce Richards.

Names: Tegart, Hiram Cody, author. | Richards, Andrew Bruce, 1953- author.

Identifiers: Canadiana 20190130903 | ISBN 9781773860060 (softcover)

Subjects: LCSH: Tegart, Hiram Cody. | LCSH: Outdoorsmen—British Columbia—Biography. | LCSH: Outfitters (Outdoor recreation)—British Columbia—Biography. | LCSH: Hunting guides—British Columbia—Biography. | LCSH: Mountaineering guides (Persons)—British Columbia—Biography. | LCSH: Big game hunters—British Columbia—Biography. | LCSH: British Columbia—Biography. | LCGFT: Autobiographies.

Classification: LCC GV191.52.T44 A3 2019 | DDC 796.5092—dc23

MOUNTAIN MAN

THE LIFE OF A GUIDE OUTFITTER

Hiram Cody Tegart
with Andrew Bruce Richards

CAITLIN PRESS

THIS STORY IS DEDICATED TO THE HARDY MEN AND WOMEN WHO GUIDE AND RIDE THE MOUNTAIN TRAILS AWAY FROM THE TRAPPINGS OF CIVILIZATION.

CONTENTS

HEIGHT OF THE ROCKIES

BY HIRAM CODY TEGART

There's a trail that leads from Brisco, to the rocks away up high.
Its called the Height of the Rockies, as it reaches for the sky.
But when I started guiding, it had a different name.
It was known as the Palliser, and it was full of game.
When Wapiti left the prairies, to fill this vacant land,
they came up in these Rockies, to make their final stand.
The hairy old white mountain goat, and lonesome grizzly bear,
suddenly found a neighbour, in their land they had to share.
But travelling not too far behind, came their biggest curse.
A yankee doodle from down south, with a gold-filled pocket purse.
You see these folks that had a dream, would travel far and wide,
to find the right mountain man and have them by their side.
Now having loads of wapiti, and rocky mountain goat,
and big bull moose that filled the draws, and grizzly with winter coats.
My reputation travelled fast, because of lots of game,
and top-notch guides and damn good cooks, with no broncs left to tame.
With the beauty of the Royal Group, and Battle Ship mountains high,
the dream of Yellowstone to Yukon, just plain had to fly.

MOUNTAIN MAN

A biologist from Ta Ta Creek, came by to see some friends.
I need to save some wilderness, to the bitter end.
He also had a damn good friend, Allan Askey was his name,
This old doc from Cranbrook, wanted to do the same.
Bob Jamieson, biologist, made a powerful plan,
we'll hire a lobbyist, to help to save this land.
We'll start in the Elk Valley, and on to Conner's Lakes,
drop down into the Middle White, of which we have to take.
From here we will go northward, to a pass up in the snow,
from Sylvan Pass down Joffrey Creek, to the Palliser below.
We had to save the Royal Group, with King George in the middle.
This old mountain was so high, it made the rest look little.
On the west side of this mountain, was a gorgeous spot,
Queen Mary Lake so pretty, and the fishing was so hot.
The Tegarts packed some cutthroat, on their trusty steed,
of the law, they didn't flinch, to do this grateful deed.
Now with the country full of wildlife, and alpine lakes full of fish,
Bob says, "Let's save this country for the youthful bliss."
We hired on Ric Careless, of whom we did employ.
Ric says we're gonna win this, for our grandkids to enjoy.
Now sitting in my easy chair, I dream about the past,
and think about those faithful friends, that fought to make it last.
There will always be a part of me, that dreams of way up high,
From Yellowstone to Yukon, and the mountains in the sky.

FOREWORD

BY ANDY

If the thrilling bugle of a majestic bull elk on a frosty morning makes your heart pound, or the thought of coming face to face with a grizzly on a narrow trail makes the hair stand up on the back of your neck, here's a read you might enjoy.

Such was the life of Hiram Cody Tegart, known to his family and friends as Cody. Born in 1950 to Jim and Doreen Tegart, Cody was the sixth of eight children. The Tegart clan were some of the original settlers in BC's Columbia Valley, with most taking up the ranching lifestyle. Jim was no exception to that trend, and he had a ranch located between Brisco and Edgewater. To supplement the ranch income, Jim also had a Guide Outfitter territory centred around the Palliser River and extending to the Kootenay National Park and Alberta borders in the spectacular area that is now known as the Height of the Rockies. With that pedigree, Cody had no option but to embrace the cowboy lifestyle, and he did so with great enthusiasm.

I met Cody in about 1969, when I was in Grade 10 at David Thompson Secondary School in Invermere, BC. I was a skinny,

Coke-bottle-spectacled transplant from the Prairies, trying to fit in (quite unsuccessfully) with the greaser group. In the Columbia Valley during the sixties, the cliques included jocks and cowboys at the top of the scale, followed by greasers, nerds and hippies. I never was sure why Cody pulled me into the cowboy fold, but I suspect Jim had asked him to recruit some free help for haying season. The deal was that I would provide my labour for free, and they would teach me how to be a cowboy. It was one of the best deals I ever made, because the next five or six years were one outdoor adventure after another. Life with Cody, his younger brother, Garrett, and a few other friends was a whirlwind of playing hooky from school for impromptu fishing trips, weekend cruising in our various cars (which we spent a great deal of time fixing) and looking for bush parties, with our ever-present bootlegged case of beer. In the summer we worked the occasional guide trips on horseback, and we cut trail in the hunting territory, where I got to visit magical places like Tipperary Camp and the spectacular vista of the camp on Queen Mary Lake.

As life happens, all of us boys eventually wound up going our separate ways to pursue our own paths, while Cody kept doing what he loved, eventually taking over the Palliser territory from his dad. These are the tales of an outdoor life well lived, in Cody's own words, with contributions from guides that he worked with and some of us who knew him best. This is also a tale about a disappearing lifestyle. With commercial logging reaching the most isolated areas, the wild places we loved—and pretty much had to ourselves—are now easily accessible. The elk and moose that used to be plentiful have been decimated by decades of government bungling of both wildlife management and wildlife habitat. This is a story that reflects the glory days of the past and hopefully offers some hope for the future for those of us who truly love the great outdoors.

Sadly, Cody passed away in the spring of 2018 before we could finish the book together. While we were writing the stories, we had many discussions about where we wanted the book to go. After his passing, I continued writing to ensure that his story was told.

CODY'S ROOTS

BY ANDY

Cody was born in 1950 to a pioneering family who had originally established themselves in the Columbia Valley of British Columbia in 1886. The Tegarts were rough-hewn, hard-working folks who, through a lot of prolific breeding, helped populate an underpopulated valley. To this day the name Tegart can be found multiple times in phone books throughout the valley. Cody's parents, Jim and Doreen, followed the Tegart path of making a living from the land. It was a hard life but a good one. The only way to put a roof over your head and food on the table was hard, gut-busting work. They were ranchers, loggers, miners and hunting guides, plus whatever else they could do to make a living.

Jim was a rough-and-tumble cowboy, in the ilk of John Wayne, who could either intimidate you with a twinkle in his eye or encourage you to push yourself for your betterment. He always came up with good quips. Once, after a few beers, while I was helping out with branding, he said, "Let me piss on your shoulder. It'll make you smell like a man!" While today that would be considered bullying and undermining my self-worth, back then it was all done in humour, and we all participated. When the kidding was done, Jim always also made a point to thank me for my free labour. Considering the amazing life experience that I gained over those years, it was worth every drop of sweat.

Doreen seemed to be the level-headed voice of reason that kept a boisterous family of strong-minded individuals together and focused. Man, she could cook. After we'd had a hard day of haying at the ranch or working at one of the hunting cabins, she would always deliver a delicious home-cooked meal. Considering everything had to be packed into the territory by horseback, she would work miracles.

After Cody befriended me in high school, I was accepted into the Tegart fold and got to know them all pretty well. Cody, his brother Garrett and I became fast friends, and I was accepted by all the other siblings as well. They would jokingly come to call me Andy Tegart. Larry, Erla, Sherri and June were all older, had their own families and lived in the valley, while Susan, the youngest, was always underfoot. All were strong-minded individuals with larger-than-life personalities, and I thoroughly enjoyed time spent with them.

Through high school and a few years beyond, Cody was always the instigator of our ragtag crew's many and varied adventures. Whether playing hooky from school to head to a fishing hole or making plans for a Saturday night on the town, he was always the man with a plan, and the rest of us just followed along. It was generally Cody, his brother Garrett, Tom Woledge and me, along with a cast of others, involved in a variety of hijinks, most of which were legal. Those adventures could fill another book.

Cody always possessed this huge store of restless energy whereby he would run up a mountain while most of us walked. Some forty years later, on an elk hunt, he did the same thing to me, scurrying up a cutblock while I wheezed and sweated my way up behind him. What I'm doing here is trying to paint a picture of the man so when he tells his story, you'll have a better appreciation of his journey. There's a line from a John Mellencamp song that I always thought suited Cody to a T: "I'm a do anything and hope it'll turn out redneck." Well, that's my friend Cody! (Note: When I checked the actual lyrics, I wasn't even close, but that's the way I've been singing along with John for years, so I'm sticking with it.)

This story is not only about a man. It's also a story about the Columbia Valley and the watersheds that feed the Columbia River. Nestled between the magnificent Rocky and Selkirk Mountains, the valley is one of the most beautiful places in Canada, if not the world. In the sixties and seventies, before rampant development changed the character of the valley, this was our playground. Tourism, mostly of the tacky kind in Radium and Fairmont Hot Springs, was a small industry. Most of the wealth came from logging, mining and farming. If you wanted to work, you could show up at one of the local mills with your hard hat and lunch kit and be working the same day. Plus, the pay was fair, and you could make a living, buy a home and raise a family.

For those of us who loved to hunt and fish, game was plentiful, and streams and lakes were loaded with trout. When we headed to the hunting territory, we never ran into anyone. We were alone with the breathtaking beauty of the Rockies. We would hike trails where no human had gone, and picture-postcard, natural scenes were commonplace, without the scars of logging. As we all know, progress doesn't stand still, and while it creates wealth, there's sometimes a heavy price to pay. More about that later.

Like all good things, my role as Andy Tegart ended. It took a little brown-eyed girl and the realization that I had to find my own place in the world to result in my drifting away from Cody, Garrett and the family. I would move to the city and get way too civilized in the new path I had chosen along with that brown-eyed girl. Through those years I lost touch with Cody, but the friendship and experiences we shared never left my mind.

Cody, Garrett and I reconnected years later at a funeral in the valley. We sat down with a few beers and talked, laughed and rekindled old memories. After that, I would try to connect with Cody every time we visited the valley. It was one of those times, over a beer, that this idea of a book came into being.

What I've tried to do is give you some measure of the man and a vision of the land we loved. Now, it's up to Cody, along with some of his guides, clients and associates, to tell their stories while I edit. I generally try to write in proper English, but I will strive to stay as close to the vernacular of the mountain cowboy as possible. We want readers to feel like they're riding the trail with Cody, feeling the excitement of the hunt and enjoying a glass of rum in a warm cabin at day's end.

As someone who has gone through many changes in my life, I'm not a big believer in destiny. However, in the case of Hiram Cody Tegart, I truly believe he couldn't have taken any other path. Cody was simply born into a lifestyle he loved and embraced with all his being. Anytime he might have thought of following a new path, the seductive call of the mountain trails would always bring him back.

School was the last thing on young Cody's mind, and, after repeated failed attempts to send Cody to school, his parents decided to keep him at home, where the bush was his playground.

EARLY DAYS

MY CHILDHOOD MEMORIES

I was born in Invermere, BC, on December 20, 1950. I was put in a wooden box underneath the Christmas tree on the floor in the coldest part of the house, with a wood heater in the corner. I grew up on the farm that Mom and Dad built with the help of their eight children. The bush around the home was my and my little brother's playground. We built lean-tos and trails throughout the woods.

School was the last thing on my mind in those days. When Mom and Dad first put me in school, I ran away, but it was to no avail. They put me back in school, but while on the school bus one day, I saw that Dad and some guides were taking horses down the highway to the mountains. I tried to escape out of the bus door, so Mom and Dad decided to keep me out of school for another year. I remember them taking my brother Garrett to the mountains when he was very young, and they even named a camp after him. I was envious and wanted a camp named after me. I ended up being stuck at home with a babysitter, which didn't make me happy.

We had an outhouse, like most people did in those days, which had been built on the edge of the ravine, so it had a never-ending hole. When we headed to the outhouse, our dog, Bruno, would almost always come along. There was a large fir tree with very big limbs by the outhouse door, and Bruno would jump up and grab the limb and swing back and forth. He kept on until all the limbs were off the tree as high as he could jump.

There were a lot of good things about living in the old house. For one thing, we learned how to get tough and survive. With only wood heat from a kitchen stove and a big heater in the living room, we learned to handle the cold. Garrett and I didn't have any neighbour friends to play with, and we were still too young to take horses and ride the five or ten miles to the nearest kids our age. Needless to say, we played well together and occasionally fought with each other. Mom was constantly washing our mouths out with soap when she caught us swearing at each other.

We had an old mare that Dad kept in the yard for a lawn mower. Her name was Ruby. She was very quiet, and during the day she was kept on a picket, which is a chain attached to a stake in the ground, then to the horse's halter or leg. We took turns riding old Ruby around the yard but were not old enough to make her leave the yard quite yet. That would come in time.

The old log house had upright logs, which made the perfect home for bats. When they got noisy in the summer, Dad would bring a car or truck into the yard, hook up a flexible hose to the exhaust pipe and start to kill them. As he worked his way up and down and across the walls of the house, the bats would start falling out of the cracks. Most were only unconscious as they hit the ground, so Garrett and I had to make sure they were dead. Things like this taught us that death was part of life in the country.

One of my chores was milking the old cow. Because I was allergic to hay, when the weather was good, I would milk outside, as the old cow was well trained. When I had to milk in the old barn, it gave me allergies. One time I had found some cigarettes and decided to smoke one in the barn while I was milking the cow. Well, Dad smelled the smoke and came and gave me royal shit. Being spooked, I forgot to untie the milk cow's tail, and when she left the barn, the half hitch tightened up about ten inches up on her tail, and she left her hide and hair behind. I'm sure it hurt like hell, but it didn't seem to bother her. The hide and hair eventually grew back.

GUNS!

When I was ten years old, my parents bought me a Cooey .22 rifle. This was my first gun, and I was so excited. It was a Christmas present, and I couldn't wait to go hunting. I headed up the draw toward the dam we had built for an irrigation system. There was about a foot of snow, and it was tough slugging. Our neighbour, Ang Atchison, had a trapline and a small shack in the area. I was watching for his trapping sets and hoping to run into a squirrel or a ruffed grouse to shoot. The draw was full of mature fir and spruce. Perfect habitat for predators. There were plenty of deer tracks, as we had loads of them in those days. Suddenly I heard a noise that I had never heard before. It sounded like a woman or child screaming. I didn't know what it was, but it scared the hell out of me. I headed for home as fast as I could, fighting the snow with every stride. I crossed the old gravel road on the high run and collapsed in the yard. Bill Fox was in the yard; he asked me why I was so pale in the face and had run home so fast.

I said, "I think someone is being killed in the draw."

His reply was, "It's probably just an old cougar letting you know that's his area." While guns were to become a very big part of my life, what I didn't know at the time was that cougars were to be as well.

Garrett went hunting one day just after we moved into the new house that Dad had built. He came home and put his .303 in the gun rack in the den. As he did so, he pulled the trigger, and *boom!* He had left a cartridge in the barrel with no safety on, and the gun went off. Dad had just finished taking a bath and was headed to his closet for some clothes when it happened. The bullet tore through the den wall, through Dad's closet and over the tub that Dad had just left, then out the wall over the entrance steps. That was way too close, and Garrett caught holy hell over it. I can't say too much, though, as a few years later, Mom gave me an 8mm peep-sight rifle that a hunter had given her to keep in camp in case a bear showed up. Some of my friends came by one day, and I just had to show it off. We were in the old cabin when I loaded the gun. I thought I had put the safety on, but I pulled the trigger and *boom!* Wow, another good scare. The bullet tore through a few windows that were stacked against the wall. As the glass flew, my friends and I just about crapped our drawers. This same rifle would shoot my first elk.

Some time later one of my hunters gave me a brand-new double-barrelled shotgun that did its own thing. I had used the shotgun quite a bit duck hunting on the wetlands below the Box T Ranch, where I was living in a mobile home that I had bought off my brother Larry. I was logging at the time and had to get up very early. Coyotes started barking and woke me up. They were pretty close, and when I hollered at them, they only yapped louder. This pissed me off, so I grabbed my trusty double-barrelled gun, put one cartridge in and slapped it shut. *Boom!* Holy crap. The damn thing went off, blowing a hole through the porch floor and the corner off a brand-new bread maker, still in the box, which I had just bought for Mom. I will have many more stories about guns before we're through.

HORSES AND MULES

I had graduated from old Ruby, the lawn mower, to Dad's trail horses. Now I was about to experience the reality of a good horse and a bad horse, and the differences between them and mules. One of my first experiences of a good buck-off was my own fault. I was riding a wild horse Dad had broken. He had rounded the horse up from Island Pond, down past Canal Flats. He had broken him for hunters in the mountains, and the horse was pretty quiet. I was riding about a mile from home when I came across a yellow jackets' nest in a big log on the ground. I rode the horse up over the nest and before I knew it, I was on the ground swatting yellow jackets. Holy crap. I never did that again. You learn if you live, I guess.

Dad had originally started his pack string with wild horses from the Island Pond area. Many of the horses I had when I sold out in 1995 were second- or third-generation horses from this stock. They were tough as hell and great in the mountains. Dad also had some blooded horses. His favourite rope horse, Pride, was one, but he had others before that I never knew.

He had bought a young thoroughbred stud called Dodger from his brother Bob. He wanted to put some life in his wildies. This horse could run, and since I was so young, he was all I could handle. Dad always kept him corralled or in the barn. He was some feisty, and when you brought him out of the barn, you'd best jump around the barn corner and hang on to the end of the halter shank for dear life. He would come a-charging and a-whinnying. He was always hoping for a mare in heat, I guess. If there were none close, he would settle down and you could lead him to the water trough safely. Mom would send me to the Brisco store, four miles away, for mail or something small, and I would bridle up Dodger and jump on bareback. As soon as I got through the first gate, he was always ready to run and needed no urging. The gravel would start flying, and I would hang on to his mane for dear life. We would be doing forty miles an hour in seconds, and many a time we passed cars going the same way, showering them with gravel.

One time I was riding him on the highway, headed for home about a mile away, when a car pulled up beside me. It was the first convertible I had ever seen, other than the old Model As and Model Ts. Well, the car stopped, and we chatted for a bit. The guy sitting in the back then decided he wanted to ride Dodger. I asked him if he was a good rider, and he said he was. Boy, he didn't know what he was in for. The guy's girlfriend said, "Be careful, dear."

Cody on Rumble, a colt that didn't take well to being hauled and, after bucking Cody off, took off for a week before being found near the Radium sawmill with his saddle hanging under his belly.

I said to the guy driving, "I'll hold Dodger while you boost your buddy on." I told the guy to grab a handful of mane and keep the reins held tight. When he was aboard, I let the halter go. Holy crap! Dodger was gone and clocking forty miles an hour in seconds. The driver jumped in his car and I jumped in the back seat. I hollered to get ahead of him, but the driver wasn't going to get a gravel rash on his nice car. Dodger was gaining speed as we raced up the gravel road. The guy was hanging on as if his life depended on it. Faster and faster we went, as Dodger could feel the car behind him, and this was all-out racing to him. I could see it coming well ahead of time. The turnoff to the Box T Ranch was coming up. Yep, just as I thought, Dodger hung a left at full speed, but the rider didn't.

All we saw was a cloud of dust and a ball rolling down the gravel road. As the driver skidded to a halt beside his buddy, I heard girls screaming. I wasn't waiting around for the consequences, so I bailed out of the car and raced after Dodger, without looking back.

Dodger raised a lot of good colts. Some were born to run, others to buck and some to kick. Dad gave me a filly; I named her Blondie. I broke her and won a lot of ribbons and trophies at the Invermere Crossroads rodeo.

I was thirteen years old and breaking some of Dodger's colts when Mom and Dad decided I should go to work for the summer, moving cattle and bulls around for Uncle Lloyd. The Kirsch ranch cattle and Uncle Lloyd's cattle ran together. Each had a few hundred head and lots of bulls. It was my job to keep these bulls moving so all the cows got bred. I was to take a colt I was working on, named Rumble. He was to be Mom's new saddle horse after I rode him out for the summer. I was to get two dollars a day. A dollar for me and a dollar for the horse. This hard-earned money was to be saved for my teeth. They were in bad shape. My sister Erla was training to be a nurse in Vancouver at the time, and she knew a dentist who would do fillings cheap. (He sure as hell did do them cheap. They all fell out within a year.)

Anyway, Uncle Lloyd came and picked up me and Rumble at the Box T with his old three-quarter ton. We saddled Rumble up, loaded him and headed toward his place, the Hidden Valley Ranch. When we were about ten miles from Radium, Uncle Lloyd said this was a good place to unload. He picked out a good bank to back into and unload Rumble, who had never been hauled before and was soaked in sweat. Uncle Lloyd tightened the cinch and I put the snaffle bit bridle on. I crawled aboard as he humped up. I could feel the tension, so I asked Uncle Lloyd to lead him for a bit. He did, and after a few minutes, Rumble seemed to settle down. I headed down the road toward the area Uncle Lloyd had pointed out. Things seemed fine, so Uncle Lloyd jumped in his truck and headed for the ranch.

Mom had given me some boots that a hunter had given her. All I had before were running shoes and gumboots. Gumboots were too hot, and I had learned my lesson the previous summer on a big ninety-mile trip moving horses all the way from Brewster's ranch through the Assiniboine to Uncle George's at Edgewater. Mom called the boots "fruit boots." Don't ask me why. They were worn out on the soles, but Mom wanted me wearing something that wouldn't hang me up in the stirrups.

Uncle Lloyd had just disappeared around the corner when I got an itch just below my right knee. I never did get that itch scratched. The next thing I know I'm on the road. There goes Rumble, bucking down the road toward Radium, saddle pockets slapping him with every buck. *There goes my lunch as well*, was my first thought. I collected myself and started down the road after my damn horse. The saddle was Dad's, as I couldn't afford one yet, and I think it was worth more than the horse. I walked and walked, following his tracks on the road. Those fruit boots weren't exactly fitting all that well, and the holes in the soles were wearing out my socks mighty fast. After about five miles, he had turned off the road, and I was unable to track him on the hard, dry ground. I gave up and headed back toward the ranch, about fifteen or twenty miles away. I walked, walked and walked some more. I wore my socks out in the hole area, turned them over, wore that spot out and tried a new spot. By now I was getting really sore footed. Years later, when I saw a sore-footed horse, I had some sympathy for it, because I knew what it felt like. I was almost back to the ranch when some people picked me up. It had been a long day.

Well, I had made my first two dollars, but now I didn't have a saddle horse. There was nothing left to do but return to the Box T the next morning for a different mount. Uncle Lloyd and I were up early, and I went and helped David Brown with sprinklers. Uncle Lloyd had hired him for the summer to do chores around the ranch. Changing sprinklers took up most of his day, as every pipe had to be moved by hand. After sprinklers, we headed out and stopped where Rumble had left the gravel road. Uncle Lloyd agreed that it would be impossible to track him. When we arrived home, Dad was there and quite surprised to see us. I was lucky that a little mare I had broke the year before was handy in the bottom pasture. Mom had named her Moe, and she was very trustworthy. We headed out to try to find Rumble again.

Dad had decided to get a hold of his friend Frank Stark. Frank owned a plane, a Super Cub I think, and they went flying, but they never did see the horse. Dad was more worried about getting his saddle back than the horse. A week later, my cousin Dennis Tegart found the horse close to the Radium sawmill. Rumble had only the saddle on, hanging under his belly. He would become Mom's saddle horse for years to come, and he never bucked again. I think that saddle under his belly had a lot to do with it.

That was one of my best summers ever. I loved riding around the bush moving bulls, eating Aunt Nancy's hard tack, and helping David change sprinklers when I could.

Going back to the previous summer, Dad, Uncle George Tegart, Dennis Tegart and Elwood Goodwin had leased horses to the Brewsters out of Banff, Alberta. These horses were used for trail rides, mainly out of the Assiniboine Lodge. When it was time to bring them back to the Columbia Valley in time for the hunting season, Elwood, Jim Harrison, my sister June, Dawn Darbashire and I went to Banff to ride them home. There were around forty or fifty head. As usual, I didn't have proper footwear. By the time we reached the Assiniboine Lodge the first day, my ankles were worn raw from the stirrups. My behind was also raw, which was noticeable when I walked. We were to spend the night there, so some nurses decided to bandage my wounds. I was so embarrassed, as they took my pants down to bandage my behind so I could ride the next day.

The following day we reached the Mitchell River Cabin. Elwood had to go back a bit to pick up some horses that had snuck off the trail. My behind was racked with pain, but there was nothing to do about it except get tough. The next morning, we headed for the Richter place, now known as Nipika. When we arrived there, Dad was waiting for us. After talking to Elwood for a while, Dad said we were going home to get me healed up. The only way back to the vehicle across the Kootenay River was on a cable car Mr. Richter had built. It was about two hundred feet above the river, and hand powered. Dad and I crawled aboard, and as he pulled us across the river, hand over hand, he told me a story. Richter had taken most of his homestead equipment, including a milk cow, over this cable car. The rest he packed across the river on pack horses. The river never froze completely over so you couldn't cross it any other way, unless the water was low.

THE GRIZZLY CUB

That same fall, a month or so later, my sister June and one of her friends, whose boyfriend was guiding for Dad, talked me into going to the mountains to find him. We drove around by Canal Flats up to Cedarville Cabin, close to the confluence of the Palliser and Albert Rivers. From that point on, there was only the horse trail into the mountains. There was no one at Cedarville, and although it was almost dark, we started up the trail that led to Fisher Creek Camp. About halfway it was so dark, we had to feel where the trail was with our feet. We could feel if we stepped off the trail, but we also had to be careful of roots and holes. I was leading, and when the trail didn't feel right, I would get down on my knees and feel the trail with my hands. We had no flashlight, so we could not make a mistake, or we would end up waiting until daylight. We got to the horse bridge, which was made from rails, across the canyon on the Palliser River. It was exhilarating, crossing on our hands and knees, knowing it was over a hundred feet to the water.

We finally arrived in Fisher Creek Camp and met a guide and a hunter there. We spent the night with no sleeping bags, and after breakfast we took three saddle horses, of which only two had riding saddles, from the hunter and guide. They hunted on foot for the next few days, as we had their saddles. I rode bareback, and we headed for Tipperary Camp. By the time we arrived, about eight hours later, my butt was worn raw. I had walked as much as I could but had to keep getting back on to cross the Palliser River, as the trail criss-crossed it so many times on the gravel bars.

We could not believe what we saw as we rode into camp. Our horses were snorting and wanting to flee, as they saw this thing up a tree about ten feet. In front of the cabin, about thirty feet out, was a big lodgepole pine. Up it was a yearling grizzly, who had climbed as far as his chain and collar had let him. Mom came out the cabin door, as she heard the commotion, and she couldn't believe her eyes when she saw us. She couldn't believe we came all this distance just so June's friend could see her boyfriend.

After the trip, once Mom and Dad had returned home, the hunters they had hosted at Tipperary Camp came to the house. They had brought a video camera with them on the hunt, and we were about to watch the recording. On the hunt, my brother Larry and his hunter had come across a grizzly. Grizzly were open in the fall in those days. They watched it for a while and decided it was alone, so the hunter shot it. They took a few pictures, then decided to go back to camp for the night, as it was getting dark. In the morning Larry, Dad and the hunters headed back for the grizzly with a pack horse and a gunny sack. When they rode up to the kill site, lo and behold, holy crap, there was a yearling cub beside the dead bear.

"What do we do now?" Dad asked.

The hunters dismounted and started filming. Dad decided that he didn't want to shoot it, and it would not leave its mother, so he had to come up with a plan. He had heard of a fellow named Al Oming in Alberta who had a game farm close to Edmonton. Why not rope this bear and sell it to him? If you could only see the video that the hunter took of Dad and Larry roping that bear, you would pee yourself laughing. The site was on a fairly steep slide (an avalanche path) and had about an inch of fresh snow on it. They took the lash rope and basket rope off the pack horse and turned them into lassos. Dad roped the bear around the neck first, and the bear charged him. Larry got lucky and caught it around the neck before it could get to Dad. So, Dad was pulling one way, Larry the other, and that bear was dragging them all over the mountain. The hunter ran out of film before the bear was constrained, but with the hunters' help, they chocked him down, tied his feet and muzzled him up with rope. As the story goes, they got the bear in a gunny sack and passed him up to Larry, who was riding a horse called Apache. All went well for a while on the way back to camp, until the bear managed to get its muzzle rope loose. It bit Larry in the groin. He freaked, and Apache bucked them both off. They finally got the bear to camp, and that's where I saw him in the tree.

Dad then hauled this bear to Fisher Creek, then to Cedarville on a pack horse. That bear hated men and would charge to the end of his chain if anyone but Mom came around. She fed him hotcakes and honey, and he put up with her. When Dad was home, he went to the Brisco store, the only place with a phone, and got a hold of Al Oming. He only offered a hundred dollars and said that Dad would have to deliver the bear to the farm. Dad realized that the offer wouldn't even cover the costs of the travel, and so upon returning to the mountains, he shot the bear. There was no other choice, as the animal had become used to human food and would have returned to the cabin. He had the hide tanned, and it hung in the den at home for years. I'm sure someone in the family still has it.

THE LONG RIDE

When I was fourteen, Dad sent me, Garrett and the Stevenson twins, Dennis and Dallas, to the mountains with the pack string.

There was no bridge across the Kootenay River in them days at the end of the park road, now called Settlers Road. The horses were mainly out of the wild bunch from Island Pond and had names like Blanco, Cayenne, Star, Panic Button and Ukulele, among others. Some were well broke, like Tonto and Pride, while others were unbroke or only broke to pack.

The first day leaving the Box T was always the worst. Getting the horses lined out as they were tailed up to keep them from escaping, Dad would tie them to the lead horse's tail with his rawhide halters. These halters were extremely strong, and if a horse pulled back, the shank or tail hair usually gave way. We headed out for Uncle George's U5 Ranch by Edgewater, about ten miles distance. Dad took the lead with the worst horses, while we four each led a few behind us. After a few pullbacks, we broke into a mile-eating trot and rode into Uncle George's.

The following morning, with the horses tailed up again, we were off to the Richter place. We took an old road above the pools and national park buildings (now removed) after we left the highway. Next, we followed the park highway to the Swede Creek trail, which is now the lookout point at the top of Sinclair Pass summit. We then descended to Settlers Road. This trail usually had a lot of windfalls, so there was much chopping to do to get through. We followed this road until we turned on an old road that took us down to the Kootenay River at a place called Cross River ford. Here we crossed the Kootenay above where the Cross and Mitchell Rivers came in, where there was less water. Even so, depending on the time of the year, this was dangerous. From here it was a few miles to the Richter homestead. There was no one living there at the time, but the main cabin was still in good shape and the corrals the same. Richter had cleared a big area for fields, and this provided good pasture for the night. We hobbled every horse and called it a day.

The following morning Dad got us lined out for Camp Eleven, which was an old logging camp just across the Palliser River, about fifteen miles distance. We were to meet him there that same day, and he was to cross on the cable car, meet Mom at the end of Settlers Road, then drive to Canal Flats and back up the Kootenay to Camp Eleven. There wasn't much for a trail in those days, but once we reached the Salt Lake meadows, it was easy going. An old trapper named Levi had a trapping cabin there, as well as many more throughout the Palliser area. From the cabin, we picked up the trail he used to travel up the Palliser. He also had horses that wandered free around the Salt Lake meadows until he needed them. We crossed the Palliser River at Camp Eleven, and Mom and Dad were waiting. We then rode about another four miles up a logging road to Cedarville Cabin. From this point on there were only trails up the Palliser.

The logging road continued up the Albert River for another ten miles to a camp at Miller Pass. It was a tie sawmill camp, and once, when Dad, Mom, Garrett and I were there, I'll never forget the cook giving Garrett and me some Jell-O powder. What a treat in the middle of nowhere.

LOGGING AT HOME

Besides the ranch chores at home, Garrett and I had to make a little money. Dad had an old skid horse he had gotten from Uncle Bob. This old Percheron mare was extremely well broke.

Dad was what you called a scrag logger at the time. This involved cutting, skidding and hauling eight-foot-long logs of various sizes to the Brisco Sawmill owned by Stone and Gillis. On weekends, Garrett and I would head out with the old mare and go to work. I was the faller, and I would go fall a few trees, swamp them, cut them to length and then holler for Garrett and the skid horse. Once she was hooked to a log, she would drag it to the landing and would return all by herself so I could hook her up again. I fell trees and stayed ahead of her all day, and Garrett would wait on the landing and unhook her. She knew when quitting time was and would head for the barn, with or without us.

MY FIRST ELK

As I mentioned, Mom had given me an 8mm rifle. I didn't have a hunting licence, but nobody cared in them days. I went hunting in hunting season like everyone else. There were always elk around the Box T and along Tefoe Mountain above the ranch.

Early one morning I headed up Tefoe with my trusty rifle. I had rounded up some shells somewhere and was ready to use them. Up the mountain I climbed, in my running shoes. I came to the highest old logging road. Our neighbour, Hector Mitchell, had cut ties up there in the past. The road was partially covered with grass and very quiet to walk on. About a half mile along this road, I saw fresh elk tracks. I slowed to a sneak and started watching very closely for movement. Sure enough, I hadn't gone far when I saw a cow elk. I froze and watched.

Shortly after that, I saw the bull. The elk didn't know I was there. As he came into view broadside, I placed the peep sight behind his shoulder and squeezed off. *Boom!* All hell broke loose. There were elk running everywhere. Down the mountain raced the bull, with me hot on his heels. My running shoes were like wings, and on we raced over windfalls and boulders. I was not going to lose track of that bull for nothing. On we raced. Suddenly the bull collapsed in a heap. He was dead and I had shot him right through the lungs. I was so excited. My first bull and no one to share him with. I pulled out my hunting knife that a hunter had given me and went to work. I thought it was sharp until I tried to use it to open up the elk. I sawed through the stomach hide from his butt hole to the brisket. Having no axe, I had to reach up inside his chest cavity to cut the windpipe and esophagus, then the stomach lining that holds everything in place. Then I went to the other end so I could pull everything through. It was hard work, as I think the entrails weighed more than me, and they were very hard to handle, as they were so soft and slippery.

Covered in blood from head to toe, I raced down the mountain for help. I ran through the yard without slowing as my older brother, Larry, was in the field haying for Dad. He jumped off the tractor when he saw me running toward him. He was hollering, "What's wrong?"

As I got close, I hollered, "I got him!"

"Got what?" he asked.

"An elk!" I replied.

"Oh, good," he said.

"I need you to help me," I said.

"Only if I get half," he replied. He told me to go find our horse Old Shane and bring him in. "When you get back, I'll come help you."

Off I raced again and headed for the barn for a halter and oats. With these in hand, off I ran again, headed for the bottom pasture. Over hill and draw I ran until, finally, I could hear bells in the distance. Slowing up, I eased into the area where the horses were. They were used to being chased home, so I was wary. Taking my time, I was able to convince Old Shane to have a few oats. Once I got the halter on him, I jumped aboard, throwing the bucket to the side. Off we went, but not far. He wouldn't leave the other horses, so I was forced to lead him. It seemed to take forever to reach the hayfield. Larry saw me coming and headed for the saddle shed. He grabbed a sawbuck packsaddle and blanket and threw it on Old Shane. Well, Old Shane was known to be lazy, so with Larry in tow and me with a big stick, we headed up the mountain. Arriving at the elk, Larry went to work with his axe. I learned a lot that day watching him work. With precision chopping, he quartered up the carcass and chopped off the antlers. When he pulled out his hunting knife and cut out the bugle teeth, I asked him why. He told me they were his for helping me and stuffed them in his pocket. Later, as a guide, I found out most people keep them for one reason or another. As we worked our way down off Tefoe Mountain, little did I know how much game I was to shoot on it.

MULE DEER

Tefoe Mountain produced some of the biggest mule deer bucks in the East Kootenays. The next dozen or so years were easy hunting for me and my friends on Tefoe. There were hundreds of muleys around. To get a good count, you just had to drive past the farmers' fields in the spring when the first grass turned green. It was nothing to see over a hundred head in every local field. In them days guides like Jim Thompson used to take American hunters and hunt with hounds. Tefoe Mountain was one of his favourite areas, and I saw him many a time up there hunting around Christmastime.

I can't count the number of bucks I shot up there. When someone wanted some meat, I was the first to offer to go get it. One winter day, when family members and friends wanted meat, I rode up the mountain, shot four bucks, then skidded them home with my saddle horse.

Dad said, "Let's freeze them so they look like they're standing." We did that, then put a small sleigh behind them in the yard so people driving by could see them. They looked like Santa's reindeer. No game warden, as they were called in them days, ever stopped in to look. When the joke was over, the family used the meat.

When my brother Larry and his wife, Heidi, bought their farm down by Harrogate, I went to investigate. In the attic of the chicken coop were dozens of mule deer antlers. There were some of the largest I'd ever seen, even though I shot a Boone and Crockett-rated buck years later. For some reason the mountain produced monster three pointers, and I still have a couple of them today. I figure it must be genetics.

FIFTEEN YEARS OLD

When summer break came, I needed a job. Walt Konkin, who was bush foreman at the time for the Crestbrook sawmill at Parson, hired me for fire patrol. He and my family were good friends, and he guided for Dad many times. Crestbrook had a small cabin down by the Spillimacheen River, which was to be my home for the summer. They gave me a Willys Jeep to drive and a credit at the local grocery store in Parson. I didn't have a driver's licence, but that was not a big deal in them days. Those days were some of the best times of my life. I don't think I ever thought of being lonely. I did get bored at times up in the tower in hot weather, watching for fires, but when I wasn't doing that, I entertained myself with many different things. Of course, fishing in one of the many lakes in the area was a lot of fun, not counting the good eating. I cut trail and old roads out when I had time, and I drove around exploring. The mines in the area were always fun to investigate.

I had a two-way logging radio in the Jeep, so I wasn't too worried about meeting a logging truck and having an accident. One day, coming down a logging road on an alder slide, I met my cousin Allen Tegart in his logging truck. I guess one of us wasn't paying attention. I spooked and drove my Jeep over the alders and landed on the road behind him, just around the switchback. Stopped and scared, I expected to catch hell as he walked back to where I was. Instead he said, "Boy, that's some of the best driving I ever saw." Needless to say, I had just scared the shit out of myself.

Another time I was driving down from the lookout tower just before dark. I didn't bother with the headlights, as it wasn't quite dark enough yet. *Bang!* goes the Jeep sideways and lands on its side, crossways on the road. I was thrown out so fast I didn't know what had happened. Realizing I wasn't hurt, the first thing I thought was, *I'm a long way from my cabin and it's a long walk.* I jumped up and grabbed the two-way radio in the Jeep. I called out to anyone who would answer.

It was getting late and most loggers had gone home, but I got real lucky. The mechanic in the Crestbrook shop was working late on some equipment. He answered my distress call and said he would come pick me up as fast as he could drive. About an hour later I saw headlights coming up the road. He got out, looked things over, said, "I see you hit a jill poke," and reached down and grabbed the Jeep by the bottom of the door. He was a big, burly, powerful-looking man who always seemed good-natured when I went to the shop. What I saw next blew me away. He grunted and flopped that Jeep back on its wheels. Wow, I sure wouldn't want to get into a fight with that fellow. We waited for about fifteen minutes for the oil to go back in the pan, then he added a couple more quarts.

He said, "Jump in and fire it up." It started, so he said, "I'll follow you to your cabin." The Jeep drove fine, and when we reached the cabin, he said, "Bring it in tomorrow and I'll check it out." There was never a hint in his voice that I was an idiot or a bad driver.

I had a black bear that liked hanging around the cabin. There had been an old garbage pit right beside it, and he would dig through it after dark. He would come up to the cabin and sniff through the cracks right beside my head after I went to bed. I would holler at him, but it didn't bother him.

One afternoon I was back at the cabin early when a car came along. The cabin was about a hundred feet from the logging road and a bit protected by brush, so it was hard to see. I was interested to see who it might be, so I headed for the main road. The people had stopped to get some water from the spring I used. There was a guy and a girl in front and a guy and a girl in the back. The guy in the back got out and was leaning down, getting water in a jug, when my friend the black bear came out of the bush to investigate. I don't think the bear meant any harm, but the guy made a run for the car. I guessed that the driver was toying with him, because every time he almost reached the car door, the driver pulled ahead. The last glance I had of that guy, he was still chasing the car down the road.

I got bored one Friday, so, even without a driver's licence, I decided to go visit my friends in Edgewater. I got in the Willys Jeep and headed for town. All went well until my friends talked me into taking them for a ride to Radium. We arrived in Radium, and the first person I saw was a logger who worked in the bush at Parson and knew me. He came over and said, "You'd best get that Jeep back to Parson before something happens." I sure did listen to him and headed back, dropping my friends off at Edgewater on the way through. I arrived very late at my cabin Saturday morning with no mishaps. Nothing was ever mentioned to me about it, so I guess that logger never told Walt.

I always liked Walt. One time he came by the cabin and picked me up to show me a road to cut out, when I had time. We were headed toward Three Island Lake when we met a fellow hoofing it down the road toward us. Walt stopped and the guy, talking through a hole in his throat, explained that there was a bear in his camper when he came in from fishing that morning.

"Well," Walt said, "jump in. We'll go see what we can do about this." We arrived at the guy's camper, but at first we didn't see a bear. Walt reached in the back of his truck and grabbed a shovel. He climbed in the camper, and out raced a black bear. That bear never once looked back as he hightailed it out of the country. Walt was laughing, but when the guy climbed into his camper, he wasn't. That bear had totally destroyed it.

That was quite a summer.

MY DRIVER'S LICENCE

I took my driver's licence test in December in Dad's one-ton Chev, with stock racks on it. After spending a summer driving the Willys Jeep, I didn't need any practice. The instructor aimed me for a hill in Invermere, which led to the hospital. It was icy that morning, and as we got almost to the top of the hill, I spun out. I kept the truck from sliding backwards, and he asked me, "What are you going to do now?"

I said to him, "Back her down very carefully, or you can get out and put some gravel under the back tires, so it will hold, and then I'll put the chains on."

He said, "Back her down slow and put your flashers on."

I put the signal light on, as there were no flashers. I backed down to the bottom of the hill and asked him what was next.

He said, "Let's go back to the office." Dad was waiting, and when we got there, the instructor said to Dad, "Get your four-way flashers working." Then he said to me, "You've passed." That was all there was to it.

YOUNG BUCKS

I met Andy in high school when he moved to the valley. Tom Woledge was another fellow in our group. Those two, and Garrett and I did a lot of fun and crazy things together. One time, after a friend talked me into jumping off the high board in the cool pool at Radium Hot Springs, I thought I was going to drown. A lifeguard had to jump in and pull me out. This was a good scare, so I decided it was time to teach myself how to swim better. I would take a log and hang on to it and paddle around Deadman's Lake below the Box T. As time went by, I got to dog-paddling, then actual swimming. To get really good at swimming, Andy, Tom and I would go out to the Kootenay River, jump in at high water and swim like hell, with or without the current. We had a few good scares and finally quit doing it.

This swimming practice was to prove crucial years later, when my dear friend Dale Anton came out for a spring visit. He was a cowboy through and through. His nickname was Doc, as he knew cattle and horses better than most veterinarians. We decided to go fishing up the Palliser River at a canyon by Sundog Creek. There was about three feet of snow on the ground, but the logging road was plowed. Also along were my wife, my two daughters, Coral and Amber, and Doc's friend Carol Steedman.

We worked our way down to the fishing holes through the deep snow for about a half mile. You could see the cutthroat trout by the dozens in the pools; it was about fifteen feet down to the water. We fished the side of the river we were on for about an hour, and then Doc decided to cross to the other side on a log to fish those holes. There was one spot where the canyon was only about eight feet across. I decided to fish that side too, so I cleared a runway to the edge, ran, jumped and landed in the snow on the far side. Doc showed up, quite surprised I was there. We all fished for a while longer and caught plenty of trout, so we decided to head out. I said to Doc, "Let's jump across; it will save you a bunch of hiking."

"Okay," he said. "But I can't swim."

I jumped and made it across with no problem, and I asked if he was okay. He nodded, took a run, landed right in front of me, looked at me for a second—and then backwards into the canyon he went. He landed in an eddy about fifteen feet down. The water was so clear you could see every rock at the bottom. The walls were polished smooth. Doc went down and came up spitting water and dog-paddling like hell. I screamed at everyone to find a pole but then realized there was too much snow to find one. We were all dressed in heavy winter clothes, including Doc, who was stuck in the eddy in about ten feet of ice-cold water. Around and around he went, trying hard to keep his head above water.

I didn't have any choice but to save my best friend. I fell in backwards on purpose, trying to stay on top of the water. Landing beside Doc, I grabbed his hair at the back of his neck, with my weak arm, and started paddling for the current in the middle with my good arm. That wasn't working, so I told Doc to push on the canyon wall when I told him to. We came by the wall and both pushed with our arms. I wouldn't let go of his hair, and out into the main current we went. Down the canyon we floated, with the girls up above us yelling encouragement. After about fifty feet we were suddenly out of the current, bashing our knees on the rocks, in about two feet of water. Doc was up and gone like a bullet for the trucks.

Carol, my wife, the kids and I collected up the fish and gear and then headed for the trucks too. When we arrived, Doc was sitting in his truck, with only a wool hat on, shivering uncontrollably. We then realized he was in shock. As my wife started my truck, I jumped in Doc's truck too and stripped down.

As the trucks warmed up, Doc started feeling better. I jumped in my truck pretty much naked, and we headed for home. When I looked back at the situation, I realized I hadn't even thought of not jumping in that river. Thank god for that training in the Kootenay in high water.

We did some fun and wild things during our teenage years. Rounding up Bill Fox's horses. I'll let Andy tell that story. Taking trail riders into the Assiniboine with Mom, Dad and Garrett. Catching lots of fish for dinner out of Rock Lake. Bringing the horses home over Luxor Pass. On Friday nights, we would pick up a box of bootlegged beer and head for Kootenay National Park. We would find a bugling bull and practise our bugles. One time I almost got skewered by a pissed-off bull I got too close to.

Another time I was riding with my friend Allan, who was pissed at his girlfriend. We were in his dad's pickup, and he was driving way too fast. I kept telling him to slow down, but he wouldn't. He hit gravel and lost control at the cauliflower tree near the Box T. The truck shot across the highway, and I could see what was coming. I turned and grabbed the seat, between the back and the bottom of the seat. The truck rolled seven times as I counted. When it stopped, I climbed out and started climbing toward the highway. I couldn't see for the blood in my eyes. I finally found Allan sitting in the snow by the highway. He didn't have a scratch, even though he had gone through the windshield. We climbed up on the road and a car came along. They gave us a ride home to my place. Upon seeing me, my family raced me to the hospital. I had broken my right small finger at the middle joint and needed dozens of stitches on my skull. Little did I or the doctors know at the time, but all the muscles were torn in my shoulder, too. By the time my finger healed up, my shoulder had set in its own way. This shoulder would bother me, even after many operations, for the rest of my life.

ANDY'S TWO BITS by Andy

As I said earlier, we have enough stories about the teenage years to fill another book. It has been over forty-five years since then, and while some of the memories are a little faded, others are as vivid as the day they happened. I will elaborate on a few.

One of Cody's favourite sayings was, "Get tough or die!" He not only meant it, he lived it, and so did the rest of us who followed him. For Cody, going to a local fishing hole was never enough. It had to be up some narrow canyon where we would edge along a rock ledge, risking a long fall into cold, deep rapids to get to that perfect fishing that nobody else could reach. He was simply wired that way, and I still have the scars to prove it.

One fine summer day, Cody asked me to come along and help him drive Bill Fox's horses from the pasture on the local reserve, above Highway 97, down to the sloughs below on a gravel road that crossed the highway. The horses had been basically running wild for a good period and were skittish, but we managed to catch a couple. I then discovered that Cody had brought only one bridle, one halter and no saddles. He, of course, knowing where we were going, would have the bridle and I only the halter, as the horse I would ride was gentle. So, we climbed on bareback, and as soon as Cody started herding the horses toward the highway, my nag took off at a full gallop, away from the rest of the herd. Though

I never did match Cody's horsemanship, I was getting fairly good at that time, but it was still to no avail. I was hanging on for dear life, pulling the horse's head down as hard as I could, but he wouldn't slow or stop. About then, he sensed that the herd had gone a different direction, and he turned toward the highway, still at a full gallop. I could see Highway 97 coming up, and my thought was, *If any vehicle is coming, I'm dead.* Good fortune shined on me, as the highway was clear, so we continued across at a gallop. I started to think, *I just might live through this*. But then I saw we were headed straight for a twelve-foot (or more) cutbank down to the gravel road that Cody had driven the horses down to. I tried in vain to stop, but the damn horse barrelled straight off the bank onto the road. I recall the horse's front legs collapsing, and then it was lights out.

The next thing I knew, Cody was slapping me awake. He said, "Good, I thought you were dead." There was blood and gravel burn all over my face and hands. He then told me that the horse was no worse for wear. Like I gave a shit about the damn horse at that moment! If I only had a gun! He gave the car keys to me and told me to go get the car and bring it down to the lower field. Anyway, I got up and started staggering up the gravel road, with birdies tweeting in my ears, when a car full of locals came rolling up the road. They saw me with blood all over my face and hands, looking like I had been dragged five miles along that road, and instead of stopping, they just started laughing and slowly drove on by. I remember not being particularly impressed by their joviality at my situation, as I didn't quite see the humour in it. I finally made it to the car, and with the birdies still chirping in my ears, I managed to drive across the busy highway and down the narrow gravel road without further incident. Cody was waiting at the gate and he drove me home. Other than being sore as hell for several days, along with a major concussion, I survived, with only a few scars on my chin, which I still carry today. I guess I managed the "get tough" part.

Having guessed that the statute of limitations is long gone, I can't help but share one more story about our misspent teenage years. As Cody was the first to get a licence and first to own a car, it was always him at the wheel for our weekend adventures. They generally involved an evening of cruising around Edgewater, Radium or Invermere with a case of Kokanee in the back seat, looking for girls or bush parties.

I don't recall what had transpired that particular Saturday night, but we had consumed a few beers, had some fun and were heading back to the Box T about midnight. Cody was cruising along in his '62 Chevy ragtop at his usual seventy miles an hour when we noticed a vehicle sitting in a gravel pit by the road, where other young bucks like us used to stop and drink. Feeling sociable, Cody slowed to see who it might be. As we got near, the car's headlights came on. I noticed the lights were two verticals on each side, so I yelled, "I think it's a cop!" Cody booted it, and the car pulled out after us immediately. I could see the red flashing lights come on in the distance.

The gravel pit was in a gully, and the road went up and then down into the Spur Valley gully. The old original highway, which was mostly gravel, veered off to the left, then paralleled the new highway on top of the hill. Knowing we couldn't outrun that cop, Cody veered off onto the old road at seventy miles an hour, sending the car into a sideways drift. He corrected the skid, braked, then proceeded down the old road, kicking up a cloud of dust. While the old road continued, on the top of the hill there was a side road off of it that joined the highway. Cody hit that turn hard, and as soon as we were back on the highway, he turned off his lights and proceeded through the gully to the top of the hill, turning off on a gravel road and slowly idling to an open space from where we could see the gully. We grabbed a beer, got out and sat on the hood, watching the cop first come back on the highway, then take the road at the bottom of the gully, which led to the Spur Valley Campground. We sat and laughed our asses off as we watched him come back up from the campground and then head back to Radium.

This particular cop was a pretty good guy, as he had a little patience when it came to us young rowdies. He was to end up a sergeant in the Lower Mainland, and he became quite well-known for his use of pepper spray during a riot. This particular night, however, pissed him off, and he approached Cody a few weeks later and told him he'd known it was him and he was going to get him down the road. Sure enough, a few weeks later, he was able to nail Cody with some minor offense.

Now, I don't want to give the impression that we were bad, and I don't want to encourage bad behaviour. We were just a bunch of high-spirited young bucks, thrilled with living and our newfound freedom. Unlike today's youth, who waste their time playing video games in their parents' basements and count their pretend friends and enemies through social media, we lived for real. Our playgrounds were the fields, forests, highways and surrounding small towns. Our friends were real and so were our enemies, although the worst that happened might have been a round of fisticuffs with either. We might have driven a little too fast or even had the odd drag race, but even that would be out on the quiet, open highway where you rarely saw another vehicle after dark.

One of my first memories of hunting with Cody was a hunt on Tefoe Mountain. There were four or five of us, a big herd of muleys and lead flying everywhere. I think Cody got one and Brian McLean shot two. Beyond that it's a little foggy. I also don't have a lot of recall on taking the group up to Rock Lake, other than I was quite excited, as it was my first trip working as a wrangler and general flunky. I can still picture this young kid, sitting on an old cayuse, frozen with fear, quietly saying, "Giddy-up," and the horse just standing there. One of us finally slapped it on the ass and got it going. Once we got up to the lake, I do remember Cody and I fishing and getting a nice pan-fry trout on almost every cast.

By the fall after I graduated from high school, I had earned my stripes and I was to guide for Jim for at least part of the hunting season. I had basically been in training for this over the past three years, and I was as ready as I would ever be. I could sit a horse well and tie a diamond hitch on a packhorse. My hunting credentials were good, as I had been hunting since I was fourteen, if you don't include my wandering the backwoods on my uncle's farm at age ten or eleven with a single-shot Cooey. Even though I had been looking forward to this for the last three years, my enthusiasm was dampened by the fact that I had just recently been smitten by my little brown-eyed girl and didn't want to be away from her for the entire fall. However, the excitement of heading out to the hills took over, and I was able to keep my longings at bay.

I recall the morning we started out from Cedar Creek. We had the horses packed and ready and we were getting ready to saddle up when Jim said, "You take Cruiser." Cruiser had been running wild all summer, and he wasn't exactly thrilled about getting saddled, so he started rearing up on his hind legs. My first thought was, *This is not a good start!* After a little skittishness, Cruiser settled down, and during the time I rode him he became the best horse I had ever ridden. He was fearless and sure-footed and would tackle steep trails that a lot of horses would balk at. Unlike a lot of other horses, he also didn't go nuts if he came across bear scent.

While Cruiser and I turned out to be a good fit, so did our first hunter. I can't remember his name, but he was a plumber from Texas. I would guess he was in his early forties; he was in good shape and had a friendly, laid-back personality. We headed up to Tipperary Camp after elk, and to my surprise Jim turned me loose with him. He said, "You both got young legs, so go get him an elk."

The first morning, as part of my duties, I was up early at twilight to light a fire in the airtight heater in the hunter's tent; then I headed out to round up a few horses for the day. There's nothing quite like the fresh feeling of a crisp mountain morning to awaken your senses. The horses were hobbled and grazing free, so I listened for the sound of a bell. I heard the tinkling and found the horses bunched up a couple hundred yards out of camp. I caught Cruiser first, then whatever nag the hunter was riding, and headed back to camp. After hitching the horses to the post, I opened the main cabin door and was assailed by the wonderful smell of fresh-brewed coffee and bacon cooking on the stove. Having worked up a hunger already, I inhaled the bowl of mush, followed by eggs, bacon and flapjacks. There is still no breakfast in the world that tastes as good as bush breakfast, and Doreen always made one of the best. She sure did know how to feed hungry young men!

After breakfast I saddled up both horses, and we grabbed our lunches and headed off. Jim had told me to take the Palliser River trail east toward the Alberta border, as he had seen good elk sign there previously. It was a glorious morning, crisp and clear with a slight nip in the air. We hadn't gone too far when the thrilling bugle of a bull elk broke the silence. To this day that amazing sound still makes my heart beat faster. I spotted the bull, and we stopped and glassed him over. He looked to be only a four or five point, but I asked the hunter if he wanted him, just in case. He said no, so we headed on.

We had put a couple more miles behind us and came out to a large basin with open areas and speckled with alders. We stopped and were glassing the area when I spotted what I thought to be horns sticking out above an alder maybe four or five hundred yards out. I determined they were elk horns, but we couldn't see how big or even see the elk's body. I tied the horses to an alder, and the hunter and I quietly stalked toward the elk. As we moved, I kept watching the horns to make sure the bull didn't scent us and move on. The hunter had said he wanted to be under two hundred yards, so when we got to a good-sized rock within his range, I told him to get ready and use the rock for a rest. He set up, got his breathing slowed and readied himself. We still couldn't see the elk's body, but I could make out that he was a decent six point. I also figured that he was lying down, and the alder was only about five feet high. I told the hunter to get ready and that I was going to bugle.

He said, "No, don't; you'll scare him away!"

I said, "Trust me!" and bugled once.

Sure enough, the bull stood up and looked over in our direction. He was in the open and standing broadside, a perfect shot. I was watching the elk and waiting and waiting and finally, *boom!*, the bull went down. It was a perfect heart shot.

I said, "Good shot, he's down!" but the hunter stayed in position for a few minutes in case. That fellow was both cautious and conscientious, and I appreciated that. I don't like hunters who don't consider the repercussions of wounding an animal. We walked up to it, and it was a beauty. No record by any means, but a nice solid six point. I gutted the elk and we covered it with brush and headed back to camp.

The next morning Jim, the hunter and I, along with a couple of pack horses, headed up the trail to get the elk. We got there, and all was good until Jim asked me, "Where's your axe?!" I didn't have it with me, so he dressed me down a bit in front of the hunter for not splitting open the sternum and propping it open to cool. Up until that point I was feeling pretty good about myself, so it kind of stuck in my craw. There would be more to come on that damn axe later, but we packed the elk and headed back to camp.

Next on the hunter's list was a mountain goat, so we packed up and headed to the camp at Queen Mary Lake. I will never forget how breathtakingly gorgeous that camp was. With the camp set up a gentle slope from the beautiful copper-blue lake, you were surrounded on all sides by majestic mountains with grassy meadows and slides. You could sit at the cabin and glass the goats up on the neighbouring peaks.

The next morning the hunter and I headed up the slopes to get his goat. It was quite a climb, but I was in the best shape of my life, and the hunter was in good shape as well. We spotted a goat and got to a point where the hunter thought he could take him. He waited until he caught his breath, then took his shot. I could tell he had hit it, but the goat took off along a trail and disappeared out of sight. We headed up to the spot where he had been, and sure enough there was a blood trail following a goat path along the side of the mountain. Initially the trail was fairly wide, but it soon became dangerously narrow. Simply put, if you slipped, you were dead. We came to a narrow spot where we would literally have to hug the rock face and inch our way along the path. We paused for a bit, contemplating our mortality, then slowly inched our way down the path. To our relief, the trail eventually widened a bit, and we found the goat dead on a wider section of the trail.

We skinned out the goat and cut a few choice cuts of meat, which I loaded on my pack board. We then headed back along the trail. When we got to the narrow part, I realized that the significant weight on my pack board could pull me off the mountain if I went face into the rock, or the bulk of the pack could push me off if my back was to the rock. So we decided that the hunter would go through first, set his rifle down where the trail widened, then come back to the edge of the narrowing. I took off the pack and carefully walked it along the trail with my right arm while embracing the slope with my left until the hunter could grab the pack, allowing me to squeeze through the narrowest part. To be totally honest, we were both scared shitless, but I'm glad I did it and even gladder I survived. When we got down to camp, Jim told us he had been watching us through binoculars and was scared he was going to have to tell my mother I had died.

The final hunt for this fellow was for a grizzly. I think we had gone back to Fisher Creek Camp for this one, and Jim took the lead. The three of us rode up to an area loaded with slide meadows, and after a bit of glassing, we spotted a grizzly. We got the hunter to where he felt comfortable, and he let off a shot. We could see it was a hit, but the bear took off into some thick alders. We headed up on foot to where the bear had been. At this time, there was a rule in place that guides couldn't carry guns. It was a stupid rule, but it resulted in three of us heading up after a wounded grizzly with only the hunter armed. When we got to where the bear had been, the hunter mentioned that he only had one round left in his rifle. Shit! One round and a potentially wounded, pissed-off grizzly. Jim told me to go back down to the horses and get some cartridges for the hunter. Great! Nothing like a stroll, unarmed, through thick alders with a wounded bear somewhere in those trees. I think I practically ran down the slide and back up again. With a fully loaded rifle, we tracked the blood trail and fortunately found the bear, dead. That was it for the Texan, and he headed home happy with his hunt. I thought I had done well and was feeling pretty good about myself.

While the first hunter was a nice, down-to-earth guy, the next one showed the other side of the coin. He was an old, rich doctor from California who had brought his daughter with him. He had hunted with Jim several times in the past. Whereas the previous hunter had made me feel like a hunting buddy, this jerk believed I was more of a camp servant. In effect, that's what I was, but his condescending attitude still kind of pissed me off.

Jim took him out after an elk on his own and found him one, which he shot at and missed. As he wanted a goat, it was my turn, so he, his daughter and I headed up to Bridge Lake. It was getting to mid-afternoon when we finally spotted some goats. I was concerned about having to head back in the dark, but he wanted to take the shot. *Boom!* Missed. *Boom!* Missed. Finally, he managed to gut shoot one that fortunately fell toward us to his death. I skinned out the goat as quickly as I could, with the doc whining all the way, and then we headed back and made it to camp just before dark. Unfortunately, in my rush to make it back, I left my axe up there. Jim ragged me the rest of the day on that ten-dollar axe.

I have to admit to not being in a good frame of mind when I took the doc and his daughter back to town the next day while Jim and Doreen waited on a real high roller coming in by helicopter. I was excited about the chance to spend an evening with my sweetie, however, so my mood was improving. I corralled the horses, as I was to head back to camp the next day, and we started driving to town. I was anxious to get there, dump the doc and head to Golden, when out popped a nice whitetail buck on the road. The doc told me to get his gun, which was packed in the back of the truck. Now, I'm not particularly proud of this fact, but I was moving real slow while the doc kept saying, "Hurry up!" I managed to find his rifle after the buck ran off, thereby saving the animal from being gut shot and me having to chase him. While the doc sulked all the way back, I really didn't care and was happy to dump him and his daughter off in Invermere.

I had a lovely evening with my sweetie and reluctantly headed back the next morning. I kept thinking I didn't really want to be there anymore. When I got back to camp, having trailed the four horses behind me, Jim gave me royal shit because, apparently, he had told me to leave the horses back there for Cody, who was to come in the next day.

I was pissed and said, "Fine, I'll take them back right now!" As I would have gotten back in the dark, he said to wait until the next day. Now, depending on who you asked at that time, I either quit or was fired. I knew I wouldn't be guiding any of the high rollers, as Larry and Cody were coming in to do that.

I recall saying, "It looks like you don't need me to guide anymore, so when I take the horses back, I'm done." He didn't argue, so the next morning I happily headed back with the horses and then returned to town, thereby ending my tenure as Andy Tegart.

While I wish it would have ended better, that decision resulted in my capturing the heart of the woman who I would spend the rest of my life with and pursuing a path that was strictly mine. I will always remember with fondness the days spent on the trails in the Palliser and the many good times. Though in later years in the big city I found myself getting a little too civilized, I always held on to a little of that redneck cowboy attitude. It was that part of me that brought me back to the wilds and to Summerland, BC, the small town I call home today.

CODY'S CABIN DAYS

When I was eighteen, Dad got a contract with a road survey and timber cruising company that had been hired by Revelstoke Sawmills out of Radium. The job was to pack them up the Palliser River from where the road stopped at Cedarville Cabin and the pack trail started. I was to pack their gear to where they wanted to camp for the night.

There were four of them going for a couple of weeks, including their grub, and this resulted in quite a bit to pack every day. One of the timber cruisers would help me pack up in the morning, and away I would go to a spot to make camp while they were doing their road layout. As soon as I got unpacked at the chosen location, I would turn the horses loose, hobbled up. I would then set up a couple of canvas fly tents and cut firewood with a chainsaw they had brought along. They would do the cooking when they got in, usually just before dark.

Once we arrived at the mouth of Lodgepole Creek and the Palliser River, we set up a base camp, where we would spend the next couple of weeks. The afternoons could get boring, so after camp was set up, I sometimes went exploring while the horses grazed, always keeping the horse bells in range. I had to bring the horses in just before dark and tie them up for the night to prevent them from wandering away.

Because it became so boring, waiting around the tent camp all day, I also decided to go with the guys to learn timber cruising. In those days, lines were cruised with a compass and chain. One guy would go ahead with one end of the chain, and the second guy would hold the other end until it was all out; then the lead guy would stop. Every so far, a plot was chosen and the timber within a certain area was documented to determine the average amount of timber in the area. The timber up Lodgepole Creek was made up of very large spruce trees with balsam scattered throughout. That's why the sawmill wanted it. There was always plenty of grizzly and black bear sign in the area, as well as moose tracks and droppings.

After working with the guys for a few days, I decided to see were the horses went. We were camped about three miles from Fisher Creek Camp, and I figured the horses would be around there, as they were used to that area. Sure enough, they had crossed the Palliser River and were on the other side somewhere. It was July, and the river still ran fairly high. I had two choices: travel downstream to where the horse trail bridge crossed the canyon, at least six miles away, or cross where the horses did. I chose the river and waded in. That was not a good thing to do unless I wanted to swim, so I headed upstream and picked out a pine tree that had fallen into the river from the far side. I waded out until I was able grab it, and hand over hand I went, hanging onto limbs for dear life, my legs dangling out behind me in the current. I may as well have swam across, as I got soaked anyway.

Fisher Creek Camp would become the base camp after logging roads were built up the Palliser. This eliminated a day's ride to the main hunting grounds.

I found the horses, and as I had left the halters and shanks on them, I rode back to the tent camp. This was a good lesson, and from then on I would always keep three tied up at a time. That was another great summer spent in the mountains.

Later that fall my brother Larry and Uncle Monty started building the road with Larry's Timberjack 230 skidder. Uncle Monty did the falling and bucking while Larry did the skidding. That would be the end of easy hunting around the Soda Springs, a small lake with minerals in the water. The following year hunters killed twelve bull moose at Soda Springs. Years earlier the game wardens had built a small log cabin by the little lake for their use. The resident hunters now made this theirs and stayed there for days at a time. There were also countless elk and deer killed here too.

Five years later I would be logging right beside the Fisher Creek Cabin. I wasn't long out of high school when I went to work for Richard and Darryn Hollowink. The company had built a bridge across the Palliser River near Lodgepole Creek, not far from where we had camped while doing the timber cruising. I was bucking on the landing for four or five Caterpillar skidders. They were logging through spring breakup, and the logs were hauled to a big landing that was built by the Richter place. I could never keep up, and it seemed that every Monday there was a new bucker man to help me. Anyway, while we were there, I borrowed their Cat and pushed a road right into the only cabin at Fisher Creek at the time.

This cabin had been a foundation for a twelve- by sixteen-foot tent frame, which Dad and Bill Fox had rebuilt and made into a cabin back when Garrett and I were kids. We were probably six and eight years old at the time. Dad had taken us along to help with packing bark away from the log-peeling area and collecting moss for chinking between the logs as they were put up.

When we weren't helping, we were exploring. About five to six hundred yards up the pack trail toward the Tipperary Camp was an old log cabin with a sod roof. This was Levi Markeson's trapping cabin and was always fun to explore. Dad wasn't sure whether Levi Markeson, Bert Scoffield or a trapper named Harry Bone had built it. I didn't worry about bears in them days for some reason, so to go and play in the trapper's cabin was fun. Dad didn't seem to worry either. Its outside walls were littered with leg-hold traps of various sizes. There was a tin stove, a small counter and a single bunk in the corner, covered with the leftover, dried-out limbs of small fir branches. The one small window over the counter was open, except for a cross rail to keep bears out. Any food, like dried beans and flour or sugar, was hung from the ceiling logs in tin syrup buckets.

One evening Garrett and I were playing cowboys with Bill's .30-30 rifle, which was the only gun in camp. Well, the next morning a grizzly boldly walked right in to the camp yard. Dad hollered to Bill to grab his rifle. We all raced around the yard and tent to find it, but it was nowhere to be found. The bear finally wandered off, and we found the gun in the grass, where Garrett or I had dropped it.

We had been there for a few days when Dad said we needed some camp meat. Early one morning he looked out the tent flap and spotted a cow elk standing on the gravel bars about fifty yards away. He grabbed Bill's .30-30 and *bang*, down went the cow—and a calf at the same time. Dad hadn't seen the calf standing right behind the cow, as it was still a little dark when he shot. He had thought it was a dry cow, or he would not have shot it. Anyway, that calf was some of the tenderest meat I have ever eaten. The elk lasted us the rest of the trip. Dad cooked up a lot of it to make it last, and he made a lot of stews near the end.

We would also eat a lot of trout for breakfast. Dad and a warden, Butch Tyler, had stocked cutthroat trout in the Soda Springs years earlier. They used these fish to stock the Palliser River, with its three sets of falls, which weren't passable by fish.

From Fisher Creek Camp (named by one of the trappers after a fisher he caught in the area), we went on up the trail to Tipperary Camp. About three miles up the trail, we came to Windfall Ridge. This part of the trail was grown over with a tangle of small lodgepole pine. It was always a lot of work to get through, as there were always windfalls to deal with.

From here we dropped back down to follow the Palliser. As you crossed Fynn Creek, there was a very small trapper's cabin, which was rotting away. Another mile upstream was another of Levi's trapper cabins. This cabin was in pretty good shape, and Pete and my sister June used it a bit the winter they trapped the area.

A few more miles upstream, we rode out onto the gravel bars. The valley opened up, and with the gravel bars being an average of two hundred yards wide, you could see the towering peaks of the Battleship Range on the Continental Divide, between British Columbia and Alberta to the east. Directly east was the tight draw coming out of Joffre Creek, with Hanging Basin above and to its left. Looking straight up the valley was Mount Tipperary, with its three waterfalls exploding straight out of the mountain, fed by Tipperary Lake. As we rode along, the Royal Group of mountains started to appear to the northwest above the Bridge Lake rim, named after a guide by the name of Gordon Bridge, who had guided for Dad. Farther along you could look up Squaw Creek to the left, and up to the right was the main Palliser drainage leading past Beatty Creek (the South Kananaskis Pass), then Leroy Creek (the North Kananaskis Pass), on up to Palliser Pass. This was some of the best elk and goat hunting in the country.

Dad had told me that his dad used to ride over Tegart Pass, cross the Kootenay River and ride up the Palliser to do their elk hunting when Granddad lived on his ranch below Mount Tegart, by the Alpine Ranch. According to Dad, there were no elk in the Columbia Valley at that time. He also said that the first elk seen west of the Columbia River was in 1950.

Another piece of elk history for this region comes from stories written by Madeline Turner. I quote from her diary (1918): "Mrs. MacCarthy, Konrad Kain and myself went on a hunting trip in October up the Palliser River after goat with Bill Williams as packer. We saw our first elk (then protected), and I got my first goat."

Elk must have multiplied rapidly, as the Whiteswan and Elk Creek areas were open for hunting. In her diary, Madeline later wrote (1926): "I went on a hunting trip with the Prusts in September. It was my first time to Whiteswan Lake and Elk Creek. I got a goat and the Major got an elk."

The Palliser River drainage was all burnt off in them days from the fire of 1847, and again in 1920 to 1922. When Dad first started hunting the area, it was mainly grass and small trees, and there were plenty of avalanche paths, which we called slides, covered with grass, alders, scattered veteran spruce and fir that had survived the fires.

Outfitters were always running into each other in them days, because they could guide wherever they wanted, so conflict was inevitable. To solve this problem, the game department of the time decided that whichever outfitter got to a drainage first could claim it. In 1944 Dad, my older brother Dennis and the game warden of the time, Butch Tyler, rode from Brisco out through the Kootenay and up the Palliser. With crosscut saws and axes, they built the first hunting outfitting cabin along the Palliser River, about a half mile below Squaw Creek. They used skid horses to haul the logs and finished it with a dirt roof. This gave Dad the rights to all the drainages to the Palliser, including the Albert River, an area of approximately six hundred square miles. His Guide and Outfitter certificate was 001. Thus began one of the best hunting territories in the East Kootenays.

When Dad first started guiding, it was hard for him to find hunters. He, Uncle Buster, Uncle George and Uncle Bob had already taken out hunters from wherever they could find them. I remember Dad cussing magazines like *Field and Stream*, because Mom would send dozens of letters to hunters wanting information and prices, and yet they would not get any bookings. When local outfitters did get hunters from somewhere, before 1944 they were usually thirty-day hunts. Hunters like Walter Nixon were also going on hunts with trail riders that they found through the CPR and through alpine clubs. These outfitters would hunt moose and grizzly in the Purcell Mountains and drainages, then travel to the Rockies for their elk, deer and goat.

This all changed with the territory certificate. Uncle George had the Horse Thief Creek area, Gord McKay the Toby Creek area, Bob Thomas the Beaverfoot, Pete Lum the Wild Horse, Dix Anderson the Cross and Mitchell Rivers, and so on. The guiding helped Dad and Mom eke out a living, along with farming, cutting ties with Dad's little Bell mill and Christmas treeing.

THE MOUNTAINS ARE CALLING

In 1979, after trying my luck at being a carpenter for Palace Homes in Calgary and living at Rudiger Ranch just outside of Calgary, my wife at the time, Marlene, and I decided to separate. She didn't like the Columbia Valley, and I didn't like working in the city. This is when my guide outfitting career started.

Dad had already sold the territory once, to Pete Burrows and Matt Matoba from Bassano, Alberta. He ended up getting it back because they couldn't make a go of it. Dad was all stove up because of hip and back operations and couldn't operate the territory anymore. I had learned quite a bit about guiding by working for Dad in the past. I had also gained a lot of knowledge from my brother Larry, plus guys like Jimmy Hagan and Gordon Bridge, so I decided I would make a deal with Mom and Dad to buy out the territory over time. I also told myself I was going to make it my career.

I got lucky with my timing, as the elk population was building up in large numbers. Thanks to Ray Demarchi's elk management program, there were elk everywhere and goats by

Cody's parents, Jim and Doreen, look on as Cody rides into camp. This picture would prove to be prophetic as Cody would eventually take over the territory from his parents.

the hundreds. Now I just needed to find hunters and guides. Guides would be easy to find from my pack of rodeo buddies, and friends like Frank Thompson and Terry Brown, who had already guided for Dad. I could also rely on brothers and cousins who had grown up in the trade. They all knew the two essentials, hunting and horses. I also had many unbroken horses to deal with, and these cowboys could get the job done. From the twelve horses Dad let go with the sale, to the twenty-five horses I sold with the territory to a few friends sixteen years later, I would go through exactly one hundred head of horses and mules.

After moving back to the Columbia Valley in the spring of 1979, my first priority was to build new cabins in the Palliser area. I had to wait for the snow to go in the high country, so I pitched in to help Dad with the farm work. I plowed, harrowed, floated and picked a million rocks before seeding about thirty acres into oats and alfalfa.

With that job done, I got a broncy saddle horse and a great skid horse called TR that Dad had bought from the gals who owned the Raven Head Ranch. Dad had also co-signed a loan for my first three-quarter-ton Chev four-by-four. I had made a deal with the Unemployment Insurance program to pay half the wages for an employee and had hired a fellow named Vaughn, whom I had gone to school with. He had been hit in the head by a tree he was falling while working in the bush, and the Unemployment Insurance program wanted me to put him to work.

I loaded the two horses in the truck with grub, rigging, saws and everything else I needed to build a cabin. With an overloaded truck, I headed for Tipperary Camp. The very bottom of each pack box was packed with cement, for the foundation. If I thought my truck was overloaded, then poor TR was really overloaded. Anyway, I packed up and rode into Tipperary, unloaded TR, stored some items in the old cabin, turned the horses loose and hit the hay.

I had already built a corral at the end of the road, which had a spring running through it and space for lots of horses. I left TR's packsaddle and his skidding harness at Tipperary. I threw my saddle in the truck, locked the horses in the corral and headed for home.

The next morning, I went to Invermere and picked up my hired man. I had told him to only bring a sleeping bag and a change of clothes. He was travelling pretty light and could pack his own stuff on TR. We got back to the corral and saddled up, and I loaded my own broncy cayuse with extra grub and filled a saddle pocket with eggs. I was hoping she wouldn't go to hogging, as she often did, because I didn't want a saddle pocket full of broken eggs. All went well, and we arrived at the camp about three hours later. I started building the cabin the same day we arrived by falling the right size lodgepole pine and spruce. I had harnessed up TR, so Vaughn could skid what I was falling. At dark we wolfed down some grub and hit the hay in the old cabin, which Dad had built in 1944.

For the next few days all went well. Fall, swamp, buck and skid. Once we had about thirty trees in camp, I built a couple axe holders for peeling the logs. These saved a lot of bending over and made it easier on the back. We could peel them fairly fast with a draw knife or axe, as it was May and the sap was still running. Things went well for about six days, until my friend ran out of weed. I didn't mind him smoking at night if he worked the next day, but he got cranky in a hurry when he ran out. He wanted to leave right away, but I made him stay another day to help me put up the ridge pole. I wanted to go a couple logs higher, but he wouldn't have any of it.

I loaded him on TR and we headed down the trail. I had previously met Ralph Stewart and Adam Pasowisty, who were logging about ten miles down the road, so I headed for their log landing. They took Vaughn to town for me, and I returned to the cabin. I was determined to get all the roof logs on before I went back to town for tarpaper and tin. For the next six days I cut, skidded and peeled logs. I then split them with the chainsaw and leaned them up the side of the cabin. After I had about twenty on each side, I would climb up on the wall, pull them up and nail the bottom into place. After I had them all up, I would crawl up to the ridge pole and nail them into place.

That was one hell of a lot of work to do by myself. It sure made me cuss the culls that used the system for an easy paycheque, like the guy I had just hauled out of there. Once I finally got it done, I saddled up and headed for the Box T, where a bath and a shave were sure going to feel good. After I had packed away about five pounds of Mom's good grub, I thought I would live; I had been hungrier than a starved coyote.

I got what I needed at the hardware store and I headed back up the Palliser. When I got to where Ralph and Adam were logging, I asked them to come up and help me load TR with the rolled-up aluminum roofing material. Mom had cooked me a nice big beef roast that was to last me a few days, but by the time I finished loading my saddle pockets with grub, there was no room for the roast. I threw it between the forks of the sawbuck packsaddle, and it rode well there. It was hot as hell as we travelled along the gravel bars. I thanked the guys for their help and I rode off.

Arriving at Tipperary in the dark, I pulled the diamond hitch and the tin rolled off old TR. I retrieved the roast, which had bounced around for hours, and continued unpacking. After turning the horses loose in the swamp, I headed for the old cabin and lit a candle. I was good and hungry, so I took a couple pieces of bread, slapped on some butter and cut a good chunk off the roast. In the dim candlelight I saw that Mom had put a lot of salt and pepper on the roast, but hunger had the best of me, and I wolfed it back. With a belly full of grub, I went to sleep rapidly. When I finally woke up, I decided to have a roast beef sandwich for breakfast. Pulling the roast out of the brown wax paper, I saw the salt and pepper. It was covered with fly-blows from the day before. I guess the flies thought they had it made with this travelling incubator. I wanted to puke, but it was all digested by then. I learned that what you don't know won't hurt you.

I wanted to get the tin on, so I built a very long ladder, and because it would be too heavy if I built it on the ground, I cut and leaned two poles up the side and roof of the cabin and put the rungs on as I climbed it. I worked it around the cabin, putting on the tarpaper and then the tin, which was another very hard job. One night, after working on the roof, I awoke to a noise outside the old cabin I was sleeping in. I didn't think much of it to start with, as I had tied up the two horses not too far out, as they were full and I was afraid they might pull out. I was almost back to sleep when about a foot from my ear, and only a log away, there was a sniffing sound. I knew right away it was a bear. I held my breath as I listened to it sniffing my scent through the cracks of the cabin wall. I had no gun in camp, plus the side of the cabin the bear was on had a small window with only plastic covering it. The window did have a cross pole nailed across it, at least. I lay there for about an hour, fretting over my dilemma, before I got the courage to go get the horses and tie them next to the cabin. Having done this with no mishap, I went back to sleep.

Having done all that I could for the time being, it was time to go back to the Box T and get boards and plywood to finish the cabin. It was now July, and I could legally turn horses loose around Fisher Creek. The grazing was great because some areas had been logged nearby and the grass was belly-deep. I hauled about a dozen horses out with Dad and Larry's gooseneck trailer, and on the last trip, Dad decided to come along. He was pretty much stove up by then but still able to ride. We rode into Tipperary with the boards and plywood and finished the ends and floor.

Once we had this done, we went back to the Box T and a young fellow from Strathmore came to visit. He was a friend of my good friend Dale Anton. His name was Dale Gallinger, nicknamed Dilly. I had acquired a good cookstove and needed to get it to Tipperary. With his help we loaded it on the truck and hauled it to Fisher Creek. We stayed there for the night and headed for Tipperary in the morning. Dilly took the truck, and I headed up the road with five head of horses, tailed up, for the corral at the end of the road, about ten miles distance. The road had originally been built by Shell Oil to access a drill site for natural gas. We loaded two of the pack horses with miscellaneous items. Having removed parts of the stove, we put the pieces in pack boxes that we balanced as best we could and then put the boxes and the rest of the stove on a faithful horse called Tag. We got Tag between the truck and a bank and wiggled the load. With this done, we pulled the diamond hitch. I figured Tag had around 350 to 400 pounds on him. We pulled out, travelling very slowly. If that stove would have fallen off, we never could have gotten it back on, and we would have had to build a travois, which none of the horses were broken to pull. Getting to Tipperary safely, we managed to get it off without dropping it, and then we celebrated with a bottle of whiskey and a good sleep in the new cabin.

As the summer rolled by, I cut trail into Fynn Creek and Sun Dog Creek for horses. There had only been trails there for winter trapping. Then I recut the trail to Queen Mary Lake Camp. The old cabin that Mom, Dad and Garrett had built had been cut in half about seven feet up by a slide. When we rode in, we saw the top half about ten feet away from the bottom half, in perfect form. The syrup pails Mom had hanging from the roof logs were still hanging where she had put them the fall before. She always left food such as rice, macaroni, flour and sugar in these buckets in case of emergencies.

That summer was the first time Tipperary Camp saw lots of baled hay for the horses during hunting season. My good friend Dal Anton, nicknamed Doc, would bring friends out from the Strathmore area, and we would pack hay and break horses at the same time. Guys like Dilly, Andy Holler, Randy Atwood and Ron Traverse from Canal Flats, and Doc and I hauled a lot of hay to Tipperary, as well as to Queen Mary. This always brought up a bet between Doc and me, whereby we would bet on major wrecks and minor wrecks, knowing it would be one or the other. That summer saw a lot of colts and even older horses broke. Doc's nickname came from the fact that he worked in feed lots. He loved this life and was a hell of a horse man. He was also a damn good bareback rider and travelled a lot of rodeos with his good friend from Golden, Bill Mercer, who was also a good bareback rider. Now I had a camp with a new cabin, lots of hay for horses, a small propane stove for the first time ever, and lights; the cooks were going to be happy.

Dad had hunters booked that fall already. There were three of them on the first hunt, and they were from Pennsylvania. Some of my rodeo buddies, Don Koopmans and Cam McDonald, wanted to come guiding. My sister Sue was to be the cook. The weather that fall was crazy hot, and the elk weren't bugling. So we decided to go to Bridge Lake together, hoping for elk in that area. We had camped there a few days when we finally spotted elk from the top of the rim, away over in Joffre Creek, on the slides above Warrior Creek. As we were glassing them that morning, I heard horse bells a couple miles below us on the gravel bars. Knowing these were the spare horses I had left at Tipperary, I told Don and Cam I would meet them at Tipperary and they were to pack up and go back.

I grabbed a few halters and a bridle from them and headed over the mountain. The first bit wasn't bad, as it was scattered high country spruce and balsam. As I was trotting along with my descent on my mind, a sow grizzly stood up on her hind feet about a hundred yards ahead of me. I guess she had heard me coming. A yearling cub also stood up on either side of her, as my legs went to rubber. I didn't know what to do, so I forced myself to keep trotting around her, keeping about a hundred yards between us. As I trotted, she pivoted and watched. I didn't change my speed or look her in the eyes. There were no trees big enough to climb. Once I was well below her and getting closer to some sizable trees, I poured the speed to my legs. At breakneck speed I reached the first hairy spruce, so thick with branches I didn't know what to do. I raced around to the far side, expecting her to be right there, and she wasn't. Now my legs went weak. I stood there for a bit, watching and trying to figure out how to climb the spruce. Fortunately for my ass, she never showed.

I now started down the face of the mountain, and believe me when I say it was one of the worst descents of my life. It was pretty much straight down, full of buckbrush, alders and blowdowns. A few times I had to climb back up because of rock bluffs. Exhausted, I finally reached the gravel bars, only to have the horses below me head for base camp. After about another hour's trot, I managed to get ahead of them.

I caught one to ride bareback and tailed a couple up, then headed back up the trail with the rest following, their hobbles hanging from the bell straps.

I was having a well-deserved rest in camp when the crew showed up. Don was mad at his hunter and headed for Joffre Creek with only a small, cooked cutthroat trout and a baked potato from last night's supper in his saddle pocket. It was going to be a hungry trip. Cam and I went other directions without finding elk, and by the end of the trip, no one had any game.

The next trip turned out better, with every hunter getting their elk. This was Mark Hanger's second trip to the Palliser. He had hunted with Dad and Frank Thompson and had gotten a small bull on his first trip. This time with Don, he shot a big six point above the waterfall slides in Tipperary basin. When they didn't show up at camp an hour after dark, I went looking for them. As I rode on to the bottom of the slides at the waterfalls, I gave a holler. Upon hearing me, Don hollered back and lit a plastic bag on fire to show where he was. He was about six hundred yards straight up the slide above me. I had tied up my horse by his and the hunter's, and I climbed up so I could see up the slide in almost straight darkness. I did the same, lighting up a plastic bag. This gave Don a marker to head for, and they started down the slide with the two little mules, crashing and cussing until they finally reached me.

The story goes that they shot the bull, returned to camp, got the mules and went back. As they loaded the mules, one went to bucking, and it bucked one quarter off and ran off with the other quarter. By then it was dark, so we headed back to camp. Don and Mark went back the next day to find the other quarters of elk meat. This trip was the beginning of a relationship with Mark Hanger that would last for many years. I turned him into a booking agent for me and later for other outfitters.

After hunting season was over, I went to work for my brother Larry. He was working far up the Spillimacheen River drainage, and the snow was already deep. I was falling and bucking, and he was skidding with his own skidder.

I took a week off in February and flew down to Phoenix, Arizona, to meet some friends and rodeo buddies, who had entered me in the bull riding at the Wickenburg rodeo. They picked me up and off we went to Tucson. We enjoyed Old Tucson and even got to watch as they filmed a duster while we were there. We were staying in Toby Atwood's motorhome, which Lance and Randy Atwood had borrowed for the trip. Rob Appleby and Ron Hunt were also along. After Tucson, we returned to Wickenburg, where we met my cousin Rick Kohorst and his wife, Debby. We were all entered in the rodeo: Rick and Rob steer wrestling, Ron in saddle bronc, Randy in bareback, Lance in bulls and saddle bronc and me in bulls. Everyone competed, but I got lucky and drew the right bull. I placed fifth out of 125 bull riders in the three-day rodeo with a score of eighty-five.

Now it was back on the airplane to about five feet of snow and falling trees on snowshoes for the rest of the winter.

There were three moose across from us that winter: a cow, last year's calf and the new calf. The snow was so deep that every day when they went to feed, they only went a few feet farther than the day before. They were still in the same area when we pulled out for breakup. I always wonder if they made it,

Between guiding and logging, Cody relaxed from time to time on the back of a bull.

as one fall, guiding in a basin between Queen Mary and Ralph Lakes, I found the bones of an adult moose scattered in a small area where the willows had been chewed down to the size of a quarter, after which I guess it had starved.

Sometime in March, Hank Campsall and Albert Cooper were going to Minneapolis, Minnesota, to a Safari Club show. They had invited me along and told me I needed high-paying hunters in order to operate properly. They recommended I donate a hunt to the chapter so that I would become known to the group. Having more goat than I knew what to do with, I donated a goat hunt. This hunt was to go to the highest bidder, and I would get a percentage of the price. A hunter by the name of Jerry Coats bought it, and he brought his friends along to hunt as well. I was off to the races with hunters from the Minnesota area for years to come.

THAT WAS WAY TOO CLOSE!

The spring of 1980 rolled around, and Dad had already booked a hunter from Virginia by the name of Bill Leadens. Mark Hanger had seen a lot of grizzly on his two hunts and had recommended Dad to this guy. Dad normally hunted grizzly from May 25 until June 5. So I went by myself and packed grub and hay into Tipperary Camp ahead of time. I then went to the Calgary airport and picked up the hunter. We drove to Fisher Creek and left with horses from there. We rode all the way to Tipperary, seeing no sign of grizz. The next day we rode as far as we could push the horses, just past the beaver ponds at the confluence of the Palliser and Leroy Creek. This area on the west side of the valley was known as Grizzly Ridge, due to the profusion of huckleberries on which they fed in the fall. Here the snow stopped us, and the only critters we saw in the area were some goat about nine thousand feet up on the east side of the Palliser Valley. The next day we pushed up as far as we could into Leroy Creek with no sign of bear. Running low on fresh grub, we rode out and went to Radium Hot Springs for a swim in the hot pools. The next day we headed back to Tipperary with Dad along, even though he was stove up from his hip operations. He could ride okay, if we could get him onto his horse.

The following day we headed back up the Palliser on Dad's insistence. When we arrived about a mile past Leroy Creek, I was looking for the goat I had spotted a few days earlier. Goats don't move much at that time of the year, so I figured something had moved them. Sure enough, as luck would have it, along came two grizzly loping through the snow on the high elk trail. They were up about nine thousand feet when they suddenly stopped. It was as if they had hit a gate. They turned

A hunter from Minnesota proudly sits behind a seven-and-a-half foot grizzly.

and headed straight down the slide at a high run. They were about a half mile down the valley, and if we were to intercept them, we had to haul ass on our horses.

I was now in the lead as we turned our horses around, and I was worried about going too fast because of Dad's hips. When I got to where I figured we should meet the bears, Dad stayed on the pack trail so he could watch the east side where the bears had run down, while the hunter and I rode up the right side to a slide to wait. I got the hunter off his horse and tied up both horses. We climbed about another hundred feet to where we could see well. The bottom of the valley was filled with spruce trees and impossible to see through. After about fifteen minutes, I told the hunter I would bring the horses around the bottom of the slide and let Dad know we were going farther down the valley. The hunter was a big man, probably weighing 250 pounds.

I was almost to the horses when I heard a shot. Because the sow was in the lead, she showed up first. He had shot her in the guts, and she was burning doughnuts, biting at her side, when I saw her. She suddenly saw me or the hunter and bolted toward the boar that was below her. The hunter shot her in the ass as she left, and I did too, as it was the only shot I had. Then she was out of view over the slide. I ran up to where the hunter was, and he seemed very calm.

He said, "She ran down there," and he pointed.

I said, "Stay right here and watch if she comes out of the buckbrush and small spruce, and I'll check if she made the timber, about a hundred yards away."

There was a couple of feet of snow in the timber, but the slide had pretty much melted off. I made sure I had put another bullet in the barrel and started tracking. It had snowed wet that morning and was dripping and melting rapidly. I worked my way straight down through the waist-high brush, following broken twigs and turned-over rocks. It was extremely thick and hard to see, with the brush up to my chin at times. I finally gave up and climbed back up to the hunter. I said to him, "You may as well come along, and we'll track her to the timber, then decide whether or not to use the horses at that point."

We worked our way back down to the spot where I had stopped the first time. I stopped to tell him that I had lost her trail, but I didn't even finish the sentence. All I heard was a throaty sound, and there was the bear's face coming out of the thick brush about knee-high. I stuck my rifle barrel at it and pulled the trigger. Nothing happened, and it seemed like an hour before I got the safety off and pulled the trigger again. The head disappeared again but only for a second. I didn't even have time to put another bullet in the barrel before she was biting at my left knee. As I tried to back up, I was pushing on the hunter. He swung his rifle around me and fired point-blank. It was over, and then I started shaking. Whew, what a rush! The adrenalin was flowing for a while. It wasn't a big bear, but it was a bear.

As we rode back to camp, Dad kept commenting on the haze in the air. It was too early for forest fires, and all the slash piles had already been burned. It didn't make sense, and we couldn't smell smoke. On getting back to Radium, we learned that Mount St. Helens in Washington State had erupted.

That summer I spent building a new cookshack at Fisher Creek and rodeoing on weekends. A young fellow was giving his parents trouble, so they wanted me to take him and get him away from town and teach him something. His name was Scott Pitt and he was the son of Bill Pitt, a forestry employee with the Invermere detachment. Scott was a hard worker, and it didn't take us long to build the cabin. Next, we were off to cut trail into Queen Mary Lake and build a plastic A-frame on the front of the cabin the slide had taken out. With two nice cabins now in place, I had more accommodations for clients.

That summer Doc also came out with friends from Strathmore, and we broke colts and hauled hay and supplies to Queen Mary and Tipperary. I spent most weekends at rodeos and took my daughters out to the mountains as much as I could. At Fisher Creek Cabin, after working for the day, the girls, Coral and Amber, would want to go for an evening ride every night.

One evening, about two miles above camp, we were riding up the old pack trail when we came out on the Palliser gravel bars. About one hundred yards away was a grizzly feeding, with his head down. He hadn't seen us, so I said to the girls, "Hold your horses in tight; I'm going to chase that bear." When the girls were ready, I charged onto the gravel bars. It was about three hundred yards to the other side, and the river was about two hundred yards out. The horse I was riding could run. I had covered forty yards before that bear heard me coming, and he was instantly doing forty miles an hour toward the river. I never gained an inch on him after that. He hit the river so hard, he disappeared for a few seconds before reappearing and splashing off into the timber. This little stunt showed my daughters that you could never outrun a grizzly. Then it was back to the cabin for popcorn, as that was our evening entertainment. The girls were excellent riders, and they still ride lots to this day.

GETTING SERIOUS

Summer had passed, and hunting season was just around the corner. There was lots of hay in the two camps, and the salt licks were full from early spring. I already had more hunters booked for the coming fall and needed more guides. Terry Brown, who had worked for Dad in the past, came guiding again. I had been rodeoing with him, Don Koopmans, Cam McDonald and Frank Thompson that summer, so we all stayed in touch. Terry got the bright idea that he was going to get his buddy, Rob Leman, to haul him and his horse up the Kananaskis and drop him off at the North Kananaskis trailhead. The Kananaskis was closed for horses, but they did it anyway, with wardens' helicopters in hot pursuit. Terry crossed the pass on his trusty steed and dropped into Leroy Creek, then rode on into Tipperary Camp.

I had only one hunter on the first trip, Jack Byrnes from Minnesota. Terry and I got him a nice goat, a six-point elk and a mule deer buck. He was a happy camper and a good reference after that.

In addition to the fall hunt, Cody would take out trail riding groups to augment his income.

The goat hunt I had donated to the Safari Club show in Minneapolis produced three hunters: the goat hunter, Jerry Coats, and two more. Everyone was wanting an elk. I got lucky right away and got Jerry a goat, and Cam got his hunter a bull elk.

Don, Cam and I decided to go into Woody's Feed Lot, which was named after a hunter by the name of Woody who Frank Thompson had packed around on his shoulders as they were trying to shoot an elk. The plan was to have Cam and his hunter climb the first slide on the left going in, and Don and I, with our hunters in tow, would go up the bottom and have them chase the elk toward us. This started out well, until Cam got about a hundred yards below the high elk trail and was just about in position. Meanwhile, at the end of the basin, a lone cow elk spotted us. Within only a few minutes, that cow picked up forty-eight head and headed out on the trail above Cam and his hunter. Thirteen of these were bulls—a huge seven-by-seven and a huge six-by-six, followed by smaller bulls. They passed within fifty yards of Cam, but he couldn't head them off, as it was an uphill run for him. Not a shot was fired as we watched them disappear around the end of the mountain.

The following morning Don, the hunters and I headed back up into the basin the elk had gone into. It had snowed, and when we got there, we found tracks everywhere, but there was not an elk to be found. That's how hunting goes sometimes. You must take the bad luck with the good. We picked up a couple bulls around Tipperary area and everyone was happy. With no more hunters booked, we hauled the horses home and I went looking for a falling job.

TALK ABOUT WORKING YOUR ASS OFF

As soon as hunting season was over, I picked up my chainsaw and went falling for Douie Ray and Neil Gleison from the Jaffray area. If I thought I had worked hard in the Bugaboos falling in four or five feet of snow, I was now working nine-hour days. We started in the dark and finished in the dark. Neil and Douie had financed four Cat 518 Skidders and a loader, and I think they tried to pay for them in one winter. I was falling for Douie, and it was always a struggle to stay ahead. We were logging small lodgepole pine in the Salt Lake area that winter. I didn't realize at that time that as we clear-cut logged, we were making great winter range.

The number of elk was on the rise, and as herds came from as far away as the Beaverfoot Range, Kootenay National Park and the surrounding areas, their numbers grew. Between the logged areas and the adjoining Salt Lake meadows, you could easily see four or five hundred elk on a ten-mile drive. My cousin Allan Tegart, who was hauling logs at the time, counted fifty head of bulls in one bunch. It was all over the logging channel for a few days. When I was falling, elk and deer would be two tree lengths away, feeding on the moss in the tops of the trees. Fir moss was their favourite. There were no wolves in those days to speak of.

Anyway, like I said, I was busting my ass trying to stay ahead of the two skidders. I would back up dozens of trees at a time, and if I didn't knock them down with a final tree, the skidder operators would. This was very dangerous, and it was just a matter of time before it backfired on me. One day I must have had fifty or more trees set up to go down at once, when a breeze came up. It broke off the lead trees, and they were headed my way like a mowing machine cutting hay. With nowhere to run, I dropped my chainsaw and tried to hide behind two small pines nearby.

I woke up in Douie's arms, not knowing what had happened. He had hauled me off to the hospital, which was an hour and a half away. I had a concussion and a broken nose. I figure my nose must have been sticking out from behind the two pines and I couldn't pull it in far enough.

After I finished logging with the Jaffray boys, it was time to go to a sports show in Virginia. Mark Hanger had invited me down to it. I was about to meet some great and avid hunters. Many of these fellows would be repeat hunters over the years—guys like Mark himself, Thurman Hensley, Louie Wood and Ernie Knight. It was interesting meeting so many hunters and having great conversations. They always had a million questions, and of course they wanted to know what their chances would be if they came hunting with me. I hadn't built up a number as far as rate of kill goes, but I showed my confidence and just needed the hunters to prove it. I was looking for young hunters in good shape to create a high rate of kill. These I found with Mark's help. I also had the right guides for the job. They were young, tough cowboys who loved to hunt.

I had a great time while down there. I met people who would use their moonshine money to pay for a hunt. Others who wanted to hunt so bad that they saved their money or took out loans. These hunters mainly hunted whitetail deer, black bear and turkey, so they were good shots and patient. Most of these guys were very experienced and just needed to get the money to come. One guy thought about cutting a finger off to get the insurance money, but of course he didn't. So now I was getting known in Virginia and had already gotten started in Minnesota. With this trip over, I headed for home.

I had no grizzly hunters booked for that spring, and wanting to keep my quota alive, I had Terry Brown come over and we used it. There was just him and me, and we had a lot of fun. I was just learning how to really hunt grizzly and learn their ways. We found a small boar above the waterfall slides after many days of hunting, and Terry shot him. All the time we put in this hunt was to pay off as the spring bear hunts went by.

Spring turned to summer, and I had my first paying trail-riding trip. Leonard Jeck, a well-known guide and outfitter from Willmore Wilderness Park, came down with his trail riders. This was going to be a trip to be remembered. I still had a few green horses that Doc and I had worked a bit but that sure as hell needed more.

Although I had all the trails cut out, I had changed the trail to Queen Mary. Instead of going over the summit with its thousand-foot climb, I cut a new and better trail with a more gradual climb up the creek from the bottom of the summit to the lake. This was a great trail for its gradual elevation gain, but there was a spring about halfway that was unavoidable. It couldn't be corduroyed, because it ran through an alder slide and the angle prevented that. On this trip, we turned that spring into a bottomless mud pit. The horses had a hell of a time getting through, and I ended up having to turn the pack horses and mules loose, which created even more problems. They tried to climb through the alders above the quagmire and were ripping their packs off. There was nowhere to tie up the horses, so Mom, being in the lead, with Leonard and the trail riders following, went ahead to camp, a couple of miles up the creek, while Cam McDonald and I caught and repacked the horses. That was just the beginning of the work we were about to face during the rest of the two-week trip.

When we finally got to camp and everything was once again lined out, after dinner Leonard told a story about one of his past trips in the Willmore. He had taken two photographers on a trip to photograph bighorn rams. While they were taking photos on some very far back mountain, a grizzly had attacked them. This is how Leonard told it. One guy was in the lead, climbing the mountain, when out of nowhere came a large lone grizzly. He attacked the lead guy first, chewing the hell out of him. Leonard lay down as the other guy went running down the mountain. The grizz dropped the first guy and charged after the other guy. He attacked the second guy, so Len figured he could help the first guy. When he got up to move, the bear spotted him, came charging back up the mountain and grabbed Leonard by the buttocks, ripping a chunk of meat and muscle off his ass. Leonard played dead again, despite the screaming pain, so the bear left him to charge after the first guy again. Leonard hollered at the other guys to play dead as well, which they did.

After a while the bear left, and Leonard got the guys, bleeding and in shock, to the bottom of the mountain where the horses were tied. He got them in their sleeping bags, pulled their tents over them and told them to hang in there; he would be back. In extreme pain and weak from loss of blood, he mounted his horse and rode for hours to a warden's cabin. He broke off the window cover with his axe and used the warden's radio to call for help. By now it was dark, but at the break of day, a chopper picked him up to show the medics where the other guys were. Everyone survived, and Leonard had the scars to prove it. He dropped his drawers in the cabin, and part of the cheek in his one buttock was missing. He must have been one of the toughest men I ever knew to ride out and save himself and his clients.

Our next move that trip was to Tipperary Camp. From there we did a few side trips, one to the beautiful Maude Lake on North Kananaskis Pass. Then it was time to ride to the head of the Palliser and set up camp. It was a hell of a long day by the time we took down camp that morning on the Palliser Pass, rode through the Spray Valley in Banff National Park, up over Spray

Pass, then past Leman Lake to the upper slides of the Albert River, just outside the park.

As we unpacked and unsaddled, all hell broke loose. The cold rain hit us with a vengeance. There were no flat spots to put tents, and I needed the only half-decent spot for the fly tent for Mom to cook in. By the time everything was done and Mom was able to start cooking on the high-test gas stoves, Cam and I had a roaring fire going in the open. It was better than nothing, and it helped dry out our clothes a bit. Wet and tired, after one of Mom's great mountain meals, we all crashed.

It seemed we had just gotten to sleep when horse bells woke us up. Cam and I rushed out of bed, and with flashlights in hand, we caught and tied up horses on the slide wherever we caught them. I had left on the halters and shanks on purpose, in case this happened. Soaking wet, we went back to bed in the cook tent with Mom but didn't sleep.

As Mom cooked breakfast the next morning, Cam and I saddled the hungry horses while Leonard got the riders organized with their wet gear and tents. Everyone was already exhausted, and the day was just starting. We packed up in the rain and slid down the steep pass to the bottom. Everyone walked, as it was too dangerous to ride. Collecting up horses and mounting riders, we headed for the end of the logging road.

When we reached the end of the road, I left the group on one of my best endurance horses, named Leo. I had bought him from my sister Sherry for a rope horse, and he was tough and loved to run. It was eighteen miles to Cedarville Camp, and there was a campground close by where I was hoping locals might be camped. That horse went into a lope and didn't slow down for the entire eighteen miles, except for on one corner of the road where I caught up to a trotting moose. Leo wasn't into letting me rope it, and he slowed down until it turned off into the brush.

I reached the campground in record time and was lucky as hell. There were campers there, and two guys I knew had pickups. We headed back up the Albert and met everyone. The rain had slowed, but they were more than ready to leave the horses and grab a truck box. Mom and the group left in one truck for Cedarville to dry out, while Cam, Leonard and I unpacked the horses and left with the other truck. I left all the horses saddled and tied their halter shanks high and dry to saddle horns and sawbucks. I knew that not being able to eat, they would travel pretty fast on down to Cedarville. After we arrived and hung everything out to dry on lash ropes, into the yard trotted the first horses. The next day was a road ride back to Fisher Creek, and the trip was over. I learned a lot on that trip, and never again would I be caught without the right preparations for a wet fly camp.

ONE TOUGH HUNTER

Thurman Hensley, a hunter who had booked through Mark Hanger, showed up for a bow hunt for elk. I decided I had better guide him myself. I already had some good hunts and hunters under my belt, but not a bow hunter. I decided to take Thurman to Queen Mary Camp, as some friends and I had built an A-frame at Ralph Lake that summer and had spotted a lot of elk sign.

Ralph Stewart, Jock and Gaston Chasse, Gary Ruault and I had busted our asses off over a day and a half to get that job done. When we got back to Queen Mary Camp, we found that our saddle horses had gone around the summit fence, and we had to continue walking on to Fisher Creek with the mules we had. It was a hell of a long day—all the way from Ralph Lake, over three summits and then down Queen Mary Creek.

Thurman and I then headed for Ralph Lake to hunt. Randy Atwood was cooking for me at the time and decided to come along to see the country, as he had not been there yet. It was a hell of a steep climb as soon as we left the cabin. We were

Cody and friends built this sturdy A-frame at Ralph Lake. A tin roof would be added later.

on foot: Thurman with his bow and arrows; me with his rifle and my spotting scope, axe and lunch; and Randy with their lunches. It was a very steep, rugged trail that was only used by the horses grazing at the bottom, and then it turned into an elk and goat trail after that. We had taken a few mules over it in the past, but it wasn't what you would call broken in.

From the top of the first saddle, I bugled but didn't get any answers. The weather was hot and clear, so I guessed the elk were in the heavy timber. Looking across No Name Basin, otherwise known as Shag Creek, we had a great view of the many elk slides on the far side. We spotted only a couple of old billy goats on the bluffs at the head of the basin. Looking down the valley toward the Albert River was heavy timber. A small spring started where the goats were lying, and it grew into a creek that meandered down the valley toward the big timber. Using my spotting scope, I could see fresh wallow holes along the creek. These mudholes had been all worked up by some bull elk, heavy in rut.

I said to Thurman and Randy, "Let's go to the A-frame at Ralph Lake and have a look." Away we went, straight down the shale slide. We arrived at the bottom and worked our way through the mess of big boulders and onto an elk trail. Filling our canteens with fresh spring water, we headed up the first slide at the head end on the same elk trail. After about two hundred yards, almost straight up, we levelled out to a gradual grade for another mile through the many slides to the saddle above Ralph Lake. The trail was very well used, with a lot of elk sign present.

We stopped at the top and took in the gorgeous view of the lake and surrounding landscape. We saw more goats, lying on the far hogbacks. We worked our way down the very steep shale slide, with last year's snow drift still about three feet deep. We followed the elk tracks and old mule tracks to a stand of larch trees that were scattered through the bottom. They were turning colour to a beautiful yellow, covering the ground with their soft needles. It was very quiet walking now, and we jumped a couple muleys that spotted us and raced away. We arrived at the A-frame about lunchtime and ate and rested.

After lunch I told Thurman that it might be faster to find those elk if we circled around the mountain into No Name by the Albert River, rather than climbing back over the saddle we had just come from. Randy headed back by himself over the saddle as Thurman and I climbed the mountain in search of a high goat trail to walk on. The higher we climbed, the more rock we found, but no goat trail. I had never gone this way before, and I never have since. I finally decided to just work our way around the end of the mountain as best we could. This took us about three hours before we finally found the game trail around the other side, well into No Name again. Now travelling was easy and fairly level.

It was about four o'clock when I figured we were above the elk. It was quite open where we were, so I picked out a large boulder to hide behind and blew the bugle. Bingo. We had an answer immediately.

I said to Thurman, "This bull is hot, so get yourself organized with that bow and I'll start pissing him off and see how fast he comes." I bugled again, and he burst out of the timber about three hundred yards away. He came up the mountain fast, but then at about a hundred yards, he started to hesitate. He then decided to come no farther and started to leave. I guessed he was getting too far away from his cows, and we couldn't get closer as it was too open.

Thurman said, "Pass me my rifle; that bull is too big to pass up."

I bugled one last time to turn the bull. As soon as he was broadside, he went down with one shot. I'll be honest. I was glad, as it was getting late, and I had already spent a cold night in that same spot previously, huddled under a spruce tree with a hunter during an all-night snowstorm. We raced down the slide, took pictures and gutted him as quickly as possible. I told Thurman we would have to leave him like that and get our asses over that saddle up above Queen Mary as fast as possible. I wasn't into another night on the mountain, so away we went as fast as we could walk. Thurman was in pretty good shape, but we had already covered a lot of tough miles.

We had at least two hours to go, and it was almost dark. We started up the shale slide to the saddle above Queen Mary, and Thurman started to play out. I had kept some hard candies in my backpack just for this kind of emergency, and now it was time to use them. Every time he said he was done, I would let him rest until his candy was gone and then we would go again. We made camp in the dark.

The next day we went around the end of the basin with pack horses, and we caped, quartered and loaded up with no mishaps. When we got back to the cabin, I took the cape into the A-frame to finish fleshing. With the quarters hung up right beside the cabin and the horses hobbled and grazing, it was beer time. We relaxed, with me working on the cape. I had the door open and was watching a couple of loons about two hundred yards out on the lake and listening to their call. It was a good day.

The following day, after a good rest, Thurman and I climbed Engagement Ridge to the south of Queen Mary. As we eased over the top, some nannies and kids were feeding away and talking to each other. Thurman had been playing with his turkey call, a diaphragm that you use in your mouth. I had never seen one before and asked Thurman if I could try it. After a few minutes, I had it figured out and was talking to the goats. A little later, overlooking a slide, we saw two small bull elk below us. I did what sounded like cow talk, and a bigger bull bugled from the timber down in the basin. I had it figured out. A turkey call for cow talk and bugling! I should have patented it, because a year or so later, a guy put them on the market as Larry Jones's elk calls.

Thurman was to return a couple of years later with his wife, Jennifer, once again hunting for elk.

MORE GUIDES AND MORE HUNTERS

Getting known in the outfitting world had its challenges. Number one was that I needed more of everything to go bigger. I needed more horses that were reliable, more saddles, more halters and on and on. I had to dip into my falling money if I found a deal on a horse or saddle or any other tack I needed. It was a juggling act to make things balance out. There never seemed to be enough money to go around, so it was "go big or crash."

The fact that I was now well known was also a juggling act. If I got more hunters, could I find more reliable guides? If I got more hunters and guides, where would they hunt so the game would last all fall and into the next year? All these things had to be worked out, and thank god that Ray Demarchi was putting elk on the ground to work with. I was lucky to have one of the best territories in the East Kootenays. Being as it was situated between Banff National Park and the East Kootenays, it was right in the corridor of travel and migration, a very important factor. Also, I had the Kananaskis Valley to the east and some wildlife would migrate from there, especially grizzly.

Cody posing with a 350-point Boone and Crockett-rated elk, shot by Claus Shulches of Denmark.

There were a lot of things that made and then took away elk numbers. My timing in the business could not have been better. Logging had not yet affected the Palliser and Albert Rivers. The old logging in the Albert River helped, only because it had a road closure. This came about a few years back when the outfitters lobbied for certain roads to have closures to vehicle traffic. I was not yet affected by resident hunter pressure, and when it finally affected me, I was able to shuffle these people up the Albert River in a trade-off, to leave me be in the Palliser, Queen Mary area.

More hunters coming meant that I had to open up new areas. The Palliser and Queen Mary areas were producing plenty of critters, but it was nice to give them a rest. There were areas where the elk and goat would hole up, like about forty-nine head did in Woody's Feed Lot. The area I needed was the Miller

While most hunting parties were groups of men, there were a few women who held their own and enjoyed a successful hunt.

Pass area. It was the northern boundary range between me and guide outfitter Chuck Christensen. This area had not been hunted past the end of the Miller Pass road, which was washed out. Ervin Morneau, his son T.J. and I cut a mule trail into it one summer. We built a fly camp at a beautiful lake that we named Ervin Lake. There was elk sign everywhere and loads of goat, especially nannies and kids. Ervin and his wife, Judy, climbed up the mountain in the Little Elk Creek area that same summer and saw fourteen bulls in Cody's Basin, which was connected to Ervin Lake. We hunted it a few times, and Ervin and a repeat hunter from Florida, Carl Anderson, took a monster bull out of there. That was the last time, as it was a tremendous amount of work to get the meat out.

It wasn't long before the resident hunters realized how many elk were coming out of the Palliser and the Albert, and the

An impressive harvest by a group of hunters from Virginia. Cody's reputation as a guide outfitter was building.

pressure was on. Everyone wanted in, and I was luckier than most outfitters, as I got along well with these hunters and they respected me. I only ever had two small groups come up the Palliser, but my guides and I were always ahead of them, driving the game away. Eventually, they gave up and spread the word.

So as the years went by, for many reasons, elk numbers kept increasing. The Salt Lake winter range had a lot to do with it, as it was open grassland from logging, and small trees couldn't get started due to elk eating them with the grass in the wintertime. These same elk, including many that travelled over the great divide from Banff, were now staying for the winter in the Kootenay and Salt Lake areas. The winters also had been favourable. There were no wolves yet to speak of, so mortality on the calves wasn't noticeable. With all the logging now taking place due to the market of lodgepole pine in China and the US, the Kootenay valley was opening large tracks of land to clear-cut logging. This was not the only area, but I noticed it due to it being adjacent to the territory. The whitetail deer population also exploded. Mule deer didn't seem to change much for some reason. Cougars were hunted extensively by both outfitters like myself and the many resident hunters with their beloved dogs. Because there were no wolves yet, cat hunters were not afraid to turn their dogs loose on any cat track, and so they treed many more cats than they could after the wolves arrived. With all these factors in place, I went big.

By the fall of 1984 my reputation preceded me, and I had no problem booking hunters. It was time to pay myself for all the sacrifices of the past hungry years. I did my own sales pitch in Virginia and Minnesota. I did elk seminars, which were a growing trend at the time. I would spend time with hunters at their homes, meet their friends and book them on the spot. My biggest year was coming.

I started 1985 with twenty-seven elk hunters alone, not counting goat hunters. I had well-known guides that a lot of repeat hunters had already hunted with, more elk than I knew what to do with and goat everywhere. It was time to put it to the test, and by the end of the fall of 1985, we had taken twenty-three bulls, with lots left over. This would be a record-breaking year. I didn't know of any other outfitter with a success record like this. However, it was so much work, and there were so many problems keeping track of everything, that I would never do it again. I was about half dead at the end of the season. I didn't realize it yet, but things would change.

For now, the tale continues with stories contributed by some of my guides and clients.

TALES FROM THE TRAILS: STORIES BY GUIDES AND HUNTERS

SPAM AND BEANS by Don Koopmans

It was the first trip of the season in 1984. I had already gotten an elk for my hunter when Cody asked me to go up to Queen Mary Camp to fill in for another guide who was sick and couldn't take his hunter out.

I left Fisher Creek before daylight the next morning and got to Queen Mary before lunch. I got to camp and found a sick guide and a pissed-off hunter. I had a quick lunch of Spam and beans and went on a scouting trip on foot to see if there were any elk around. I climbed the ridge behind the cabin, into No Name Basin, then into Rolfe Lake. Keeping my elevation in the rock bluffs above Rolfe Lake, I made it onto the ridge looking down into Donnie's Basin. I got to the top of the ridge and looked down to see six bull elk and a bunch of cows. There were a few smaller bulls, a nice six point and one very big one. I wanted to stay and glass them for a while but had to get back to Queen Mary before dark. I got back to camp in time for more Spam and beans and told the hunter to rest up because we were going on a long hike the next day. I told him about the elk I had spotted, and his mood improved a lot.

Don Koopmans and Miss the mule with a 346 ⅞-rated Boone and Crockett bull elk, which garnered the Southern British Columbia Guides and Outfitters trophy in 1984.

We got up early the next day and packed up Miss, the smallest but toughest mule I had ever seen. I told the hunter to take all his stuff, as we might not be back. I found out he was a sergeant in the US Army, and he looked tough enough. We left at daylight and retraced my steps from the day before. Crossing the rock bluffs above Rolfe Lake had been much easier without a hunter and a mule. More than once I was afraid the mule, or the hunter for that matter, would lose their footing and fall down the mountain. We made it to the ridge looking down into Donnie's Basin and crept over the top, hoping to see all the elk waiting for us. We saw nothing—not a thing, and the hunter was pissed off again.

"Well," I said, "they must be in the timber on the other side of the basin." We slid our way down to the basin, crossed the bottom and found an elk trail up the other side. By now my hunter was getting tired and hanging onto Miss's tail to help pull him up the steeper parts. We were halfway up the other side, taking a break.

The hunter asked, "Where's the elk?"

I said, "Beats me. Do you want to see Tipperary Camp?" He asked where that camp was. I told him it was just over the ridge and down the creek, not that far. He asked if they had Spam and beans there. I told him I didn't think so.

He said, "Let's go." We climbed the rest of the way to the top, with the hunter hanging off the tail of the mule. Now we were on the ridge between Donnie's Basin and Squaw Creek. The hunter came up beside me and asked where the camp was.

I told him, "It's just down there at the mouth of Squaw Creek." It was quite steep going down at first, and when we hit the timber at the bottom, it was hard going, as we couldn't find any elk trails to help us. We bushwhacked our way until we found the old pack trails that would lead us to camp. At one creek crossing the hunter thought he should get a ride across on the mule. He climbed on her back on top of the pack. She waited till she was in the middle of the creek and bucked him off. I guess that was her payback for pulling him up the mountain. I kind of laughed to myself. We made it to Tipperary Camp just after dark. Cody was there and asked where in the hell we had come from. When I told him, he couldn't believe it. We fed Miss some oats, but she was too tired to even eat. She just stood and stared at it. I'm not sure what we had for supper, but I'm sure it wasn't Spam and beans.

After a good night's sleep, I took the hunter to the Waterfall Basin and shot a very small three-point elk. After the way the hunter's trip had gone so far, he was quite happy to have it.

For my second trip in 1984, Cody lined me up with a hunter from Virginia by the name of Richard, I think. I still had the big bull that I had seen the trip before in Donnie's Basin in my mind, and I asked Cody if I could go back to Queen Mary and see if he was still around. Not many volunteered to go to that camp, so of course he agreed. We saddled our horses and packed our groceries and duffle on Miss, my favourite mule. We got to camp in good time and went to bed early, knowing we had a long day ahead of us.

The next morning we packed up the mule and left on foot into Rolfe Lake, where we planned to camp for a couple of nights in a pup tent and cook over an open fire. We got to Rolfe Lake around lunchtime, and after setting up our tent and having a bite to eat, we decided to climb the ridge and have a look into Donnie's Basin. After a couple hours of climbing, we got to the top of the ridge and settled in to start glassing the basin, looking for the big one. We had sat for maybe five minutes when we heard a bull bugle way up the other side. We watched for a few minutes, then saw the big bull chasing a cow at full speed down an elk trail, all the way to the bottom.

I told Richard if we hurried, we could get to the bottom and have a chance at him before dark. Away we went, as fast as we could, trying to stay out of sight and not make too much noise. We got to the bottom, where we could still hear the bull bugling and had a good idea about where he was. The bull was preoccupied with his cow, and we got to around two hundred yards from them. Richard got set up on a rest and downed the bull with one shot. We walked up to where he fell and realized that we had a very nice bull on our hands. Now reality set in. We were three hours from our camp, and it was less than two hours till dark. I asked Richard where he wanted to sleep, beside the elk or in the pup tent. He decided on the pup tent, so we left the elk and began our hike back up the ridge and down into Rolfe Lake.

We saw grizzly tracks over top of ours as we started down toward camp. I was a bit worried about our tent and Miss, who was tied up close to the tent. The grizzly had circled the tent but thankfully didn't bother anything. I remember as I was frying something up for dinner that Richard thought it was healthy to skip a meal every now and then and that tonight might be a good night to skip one.

The next morning we took Miss with us and went back to the elk, hoping the bears had not found it. After a three-hour hike we came to the elk to find it just like we had left it the night before. I took the cape, Richard took the horns and Miss packed the boned-out meat back to our camp. It was a long, hard day, but it was worth it when we finally made it back.

We spent another night in the pup tent, hoping the bears didn't follow the fresh meat to camp. After a cold night in the tent, we packed up and left for Queen Mary and arrived around suppertime. I put the mule away while Richard made dinner. We ate a whole canned chicken and canned spuds. It was one of the best meals I've ever had. After a good meal and a night in a warm cabin, we packed up and went back to Fisher Creek to catch up with Cody and his hunter. The elk scored 346 ⅞ and was good enough to win the Southern British Columbia Guides and Outfitters trophy for the largest elk taken that year.

TEXAS TIM AND PENDEJO by Texas Tim

Pendejo and I started working for Cody in the early nineties. I believe it was in the spring, and we would work for him that summer as well. Sometime along there we had a bunch of older people who wanted to go up with him to Sylvan Pass. When the time came for the great journey, they all showed up with little silky packages that weighed about ten pounds each, which we were supposed to pack into mannys, which are bundles you can put in a mule's two packs. Packing all these little silky bundles was like trying to stuff balloons into an open-ended pillowcase. You would stick one in and the other one would pop out. It was the damnedest shit I ever saw in my life. Anyway, we got several mannys made up and a couple of mules packed. We had sent the pilgrims on up the mountain trail while we were packing. We didn't know who was leading them, but they were all on foot, and our plan was to follow along later.

As I said previously, they were older, and there was one lady in her late seventies who'd had several hip operations and had crutches. I have no idea how she thought she was going to climb that mountain, but to her credit she made it about halfway up. It was a rough trail, and there was about a hundred yards of three-foot-deep mud for the horses and mules to get through, plus a hundred yards of boulders as big as refrigerators that we had to crawl over. There had been a slide earlier in the spring, so we tried to fill up the gaps between the rocks with smaller rocks so the mules and horses could get across it. It was a real mess.

Anyway, we got about halfway up with the pack string to where this older lady had stopped. She simply couldn't go any farther. I couldn't load her on Pendejo, as he didn't like

Texas Tim and his mule, Pendejo, (right) began working for Cody, here on Jake (left), in the early nineties.

anybody on him but me. However, Darryl McLean had an old paint horse named Chief that was an evil old bastard but semi-gentle, so we loaded her up. I was going to lead Chief, and Darryl was going to walk along beside and hold on to the woman because, as I said, she was on double crutches. We got her loaded up, which was quite an ordeal, as her feet couldn't reach the stirrups. She was sitting up there like a watermelon and holding onto the saddle horn while I led old Chief. Meanwhile, Chief would bite Pendejo in the ass and then Pendejo would kick him in the chest. Chief would pull back, then lunge forward. The old woman would scream like a wildcat every time the horse moved. We went on for miles like that, with Chief biting Pendejo, then Pendejo kicking the shit out of him and Chief hauling back, with this old woman screaming. This went on for hours, and I was worn to a frazzle by the time we got there. I'm sure she was, too, and though she didn't fall off, it sure wasn't for lack of trying. We finally made it up there, and all these pilgrims were spread out under their umbrellas.

Some lady had lost her sleeping bag somewhere. It had either been left in the car or had punched out of one of the mannys on the way up. Oh my god! It was about twenty miles back to the car. Cody and I headed back down with the pack string and found the bag right down in the middle of that god-awful bog. Cody said I would have to take the bag back up there again.

I said, "Bullshit, she can crawl into somebody else's sleeping bag! Pendejo is done. He's already been up there and back today; it must be fifteen miles back up there."

I can't remember what Cody offered me, but it must have been worthwhile, so I grabbed the sleeping bag and headed back up. Pendejo was madder than shit. There ain't nothing worse than riding a mule in the wrong direction where he doesn't want to go. It seemed to take forever, but we got up there and she was so glad to see her sleeping bag. She had a pint of rum and offered me a sip. Well, if you're going to offer me a sip of something after I ride fifteen miles out of my way, you won't get much back. Anyway, I got me a good whammy of that rum. Me and Cody had hauled some bales and oats up there a few days before, so I unpacked Pendejo and gave him a good meal before we headed back down. I got back down to base about midnight or so. I was played right out and could hardly move. The deal had got done!

The group called down the next day and said someone had to get hauled out by a helicopter. Me and Cody had to go back up there and somehow get that crap arranged and pack up all their shit. They might have at least stayed a few days. We headed up there, got them organized and on a helicopter. I don't know what that cost them and I don't care. A few days later we packed up all their crap, and heading back down, I didn't care how much stuff fell off. I don't think we lost much. Cody made a million dollars off the deal, and Pendejo and I felt like we damn near killed each other making that journey two times in one day.

There would be several more adventures that year with Cody. A million things come to mind, but that was one of the weirdest ones by far.

MY GUIDING EXPERIENCES by Ervin Morneau

I came from New Brunswick in 1979. I had only used horses for logging, garden work and haying. When I met Cody Tegart in the summer of 1980, he took me out to learn to pack horses and mules, and how to cut trail and build cabins (as I am a carpenter). That same fall Cody asked me to guide hunters for him, as I love to hunt.

My first hunt is from Tipperary Cabin with a man named Gary, along with Frank Thompson and his hunter. We get up early, saddle horses, eat breakfast, then head out. As we head up back, we hear an elk bugle. I ask, "Can I go after him?"

Frank says no, that's Lorne's area. We ride and hear another bugle. I ask the same question and he says no, that's Don Koopman's area. So, we ride on and yet again hear another bugle. This time it's Larry Tegart's area. So we go up to the Grizzly Ridge, Beatty Creek area. This is Frank's domain for the day. He clues me in on my apprenticeship. Glass and watch,

Ervin Morneau (right, back) and Darryl McLean (right, front) guided for Cody on a regular basis.

snack, then watch, glass and watch, eat. This goes on all day and nothing shows. On the way back, about a half mile from camp and across the river, we hear another bull bugle. I ask Frank, "Whose area is this?"

Franks says, "That's nobody's area. It's a hellhole with very thick and heavy alders."

I say, "Frank, will you ride Gary and me over there in the morning?" He agrees, probably to teach the rookie a lesson.

Next morning, same routine, except Gary and I get a ride over and within twenty minutes we hear the bull bugling. Frank was right. The alders were very thick, and it was noisy and rainy. The bull and I are having a very good talk through the bush and deadfall. I tell Gary we can't get at him, so please take off that noisy rain gear and we will crawl through the alders where the bears go through. He tells me we will not be able to find his gear later. He's probably thinking that being as I am a rookie, I suppose, but I tell him no problem. So, we crawl through alders while the bull and I have a chat. We come out in a small opening and stand up. Gary asks if I see the bull.

I answer, "Yes, he is right above us, about fifty feet away." This is where the "fun" starts. I tell Gary to shoot, then I see him put his gun up and aim, then put it down.

"What's the matter?" He tells me his scope is fogged. Still doing cow talk to the bull, I give Gary my hanky (not used!), and he cleans his scope, aims and fires. The bull tumbles down from us and ends up with one horn under a large spruce root. I tell Gary to shoot him again because the bull is trying to get up. He informs me he can't see the bull in his scope. This rookie is getting pretty excited! I take a hold of the barrel of the gun and place it on the head of the elk and tell him to pull the trigger. Gary does, and the bull is finished.

We do the congratulations, high-five and get pictures, then I go to caping out the head and quartering the elk. When I cape him out I see a piece of horn, up a couple of inches from the skull, is missing. Then when I finish dressing out the rest of the elk, I do not find a bullet hole except the one in the head. If it were not for the bull getting his horn stuck under the root, we would have not had bragging rights.

Next day is when the hunter and I learn how to pack my first elk out with mules. It was a very good experience, with many more in years to come.

This next story is about a great hunter from Florida named Carl Anderson. I had him eight or more times with Cody and twice with Mike Christian.

On this hunt we are at Tipperary Cabin. We hunt up the back end of the Palliser River and spot four mule deer bucks up Beauty Creek area. We hike up after them and get in range of two big non-typical and two four points. We decide on the larger non-typical. Carl takes aim and misses. I tell him he is shooting low. He fires twice, and I think I see blood fly, but they keep going out of sight. I climb up to see them still trailing. I look for blood but discover what Carl hit was a rotten red log, no deer.

The next day we go up Squaw Creek, and about 10:30 or 11 o'clock we hear horn crackling. We tie up the horses and hurry closer to see two six-point bulls fighting at about 250 to 300 yards away uphill. I tell Carl to take one when they stop. He tells me after yesterday, with the mule deer, he wants to get closer. So we go back down and around. I don't expect them to still be there when we finally get around to the other side. But as luck would have it, one bull is standing in the open, and the other is ready to walk into the alders. Carl leans on a tree and fires. The bull jumps, then crashes into the brush. I tell Carl to stay where he is while I head up to find him. He tells me to go in at a certain spot to find his elk. I can't find it.

Then Carl yells, "Ervin, you chased him back out!"

I yell for him to shoot. He fires, and I hear the bull come crashing through the brush toward me. Then it stops, so I head toward it and there it is, dead. I say to myself, *This is not the bull he first shot at.* So I look around some more and sure enough, thirty or forty feet away lies another bull, both of them six points. Carl comes up and I tell him what happened.

He says. "No, I couldn't even hit a mule deer yesterday."

So I tell him, "I don't have to hunt for myself later; I'll just tag one of these."

I have another story about an adventure I shared with Carl Anderson.

We pack up the two mules, Whiskey and Bourbon, and head up into the new country and Ervin Lake. We see elk at daybreak every day, but it is very hot, so they vanish at first light. This happens for several days. Carl loves to get his game, but he also just loves to be out in the backcountry. There are three days left of the hunt, and food is getting down. I kill two grouse with rocks, so when we get back to our lean-to adobe, I start to build a stew.

I hear Carl say something and ask what he said. He says that a mule is loose from her tether—but these two mules are very close, so if one is loose, the other will work hard to be loose also. I run over just as Whiskey decides his partner, Bourbon, is too far away from him—ten feet—so he goes back into a run toward her and breaks the lash rope. I run up the hill ahead of them to head them off, but as luck would have it, they get past me. So I run for the pass to head them off. When I reach it, they are eating in the meadow below me, as it was a high climb to the pass. I am burned out, so I just watch them for ten or so minutes while I get my breath back and think over the problem.

On the way in we have two other lean-to areas at which to camp. At the first one, there is a drop-off gorge and a rock wall straight up. So I figure if I call them and run to keep ahead, I may be able to catch one at the gorge. I call them, and right away they come running. I take off running ahead of them about three hundred yards. I look back and here they come. I holler and run down the hill again. I run past a high goat trail and keep running. Then suddenly, I can't hear them behind me. I stop, look back and there is no sign of them. I think they might be heading back, as this is their first time in this area. I then hear a rock fall from above.

I look way up and there they are, up where the goats belong. I'm thinking, *When and if I catch you guys, I'll take you anywhere to carry out elk.* I yell to Whiskey and Bourbon; they realize they missed the trail, then head straight down the mountain. So I take off running to keep ahead. We had just passed camp two, and I don't want them ahead of me, so I jog all the way back and see them about fifty yards away. I notice their halter shanks hanging over their ears. I think when they get close, I'll rub my hands together to get them closer and hope to catch a halter without one of them pulling back and causing me to fall in the canyon. They come closer. I reach for the halter shank and Whiskey just stands there. I think they had enough of this silly game.

We head back to camp three again. We get back and Carl leaves me a note that he will be sitting on a knoll where we sat a few times before. I eat, then head over. When I get there, the sun is hot. I take off my boots and socks and hang them to dry. I lie back for a snooze. I just close my eyes and then look at Carl and say, "Please tell me I did not just hear that."

He says, "Yes Ervin, that was an elk bugle." About a mile away, I spot a large yellow object and a cow a while later. The sun silhouettes them, so we head after them. He was bugling well when we left, but when we get to the lake, he stops bugling. We sit in the trees and Carl pulls out a book.

I say, "Are you speed reading?" He turned the pages so fast.

He says, "When are we going to go?"

I say, "When he tells me where he is." The elk roars out a bugle, then we head for it. We come out in the open by the lake.

I say we better get into the trees and as we go to the trees, the cow comes running down the trail. When the cow is fifty feet away, I ask Carl if he sees the bull.

He says, "Yes, and he is a legal six-by-six!" I tell him to shoot, which he does. The cow runs by, but the bull just stands there. So, I say shoot again, and the same thing. I say shoot again. Carl says he is dead. I ask if he is shooting a different bull than I'm seeing? That's when I see the bullet holes and blood coming out his nose. He then falls over dead. We do all the high-fives and take pictures, then we go to work preparing for hauling out. We look up on a high ledge and there is a big billy goat.

I say, "Carl I don't want to take the moment away, but we could get your goat also. The elk is finished being cut up."

He says, "Let's try," so we go to the edge of lake about four hundred yards uphill to the goat. Carl says, "I'll use a log for a rest." So, he lays down, aims and fires. Then he bellows, "Scope bite!"

I am spotting the goat at that time. The bullet hit six inches above the goat. I think it scared him so bad he just froze still. I look at Carl, and he is pouring blood under his eye. I give him my handkerchief, and we put ice-cold water on it, and it stops in awhile. It needs stitches, but a band-aid will have to do.

The next day we bring the mules in early, around four o'clock. Carl thought a grizzly might get his meat, and Carl loves elk.

We load up and head out for a two-day trip. When we make the road where the truck and trailer are, the first person we meet is a paramedic. He cleans Carl's eye wound but says it should have had stitches. Like that would happen up on the mountain with no painkiller, and Carl with a gun. The medic says it needs to dry out now and to do it on the way to base camp. We decide to make up a story about Carl's black eye and cut.

The first person we see is Cody's wife, Linda. She says, "Carl, what happened to your eye?"

Then Carl, straight-faced, tells her the story of shooting the elk twice and me saying to shoot again, as it was still standing. He says, "I say to Ervin, 'No, he is already dead. I will not shoot again.' So Ervin backhanded me."

Linda hollers, "Ervin, you cannot do that!"

I say, "Are you the guide or me?"

She is a little angry when Carl bursts out laughing.

I've got one more tale to tell, and it's about a black bear. It was December 15, hunting season was over, and Cody, Terry Brown and I decided we needed a few Christmas trees.

We take my pickup and head out up on the mountain above Cody's dad's. We are driving some logging roads when a yearling black bear runs down the road and up a tree. There is about a foot of snow. We had a few good-idea beers, so we decide to cut this small tree down and catch the bear. Cody cuts the tree, and Terry and I catch the bear from the back and front. We put him in the back of the truck with the cap on it. Then we have a beer and decide to put him in my chicken house. I put in food and water for him. We call him Theodor.

Late in January I am coming home from work when I spot Theodor loose at the end of my driveway. Panic mode kicks in, and I chase him up a tree near the highway, which, fortunately, was not too busy back in the eighties. I climb the tree with a rope, and as I reach to tie him, he tries to bite me. After a few attempts I decide I need help, so I go down and get my son T.J. As I get to the ground, so does the bear. I'm in panic mode again! I don't need Theodor roaming around Brisco. I chase him back up the tree.

I'm angry now—not at the bear, but at my son, whose job it is to feed the bear. I get up the tree and reach for the bear with my left hand, and he tries to bite me. I punch him in the nose with my right hand. He goes groggy, and I tie him by the back leg and take him down the tree. I try to put him in the back of my truck, but he gets too lively, so I tie him to the bumper and head one kilometre. I yell for T.J. to help, and I tell him he left the door open.

He says, "No, Dad, I didn't." He runs on ahead and when I bring Theodor, he opens the door and says, "I don't like to tell you, but Theodor is in here lying in the hay."

It turned out the new bear was very hungry. We fed both bears till about mid-April and then let them go. I would continue to see Theodor for six years on the mountain above us. I could tell it was him by the big white *V* on his shoulder and chest.

THE PALLISER RIVER TRIP by Dr. Irvin Hess

In September of 1990, my friend Mike Hill and I left on our long-awaited hunting trip. We travelled to Washington, DC, where we met with the other members of our hunting party: J.D. McCurdy, Louie Kugler and Larry Carpenter. We flew to Salt Lake City and then to Calgary, finally ending at our destination of Cranbrook, BC. That night at our motel, there were five of us and only bed space for four, so Mike and I alternated sleeping on the floor. From that night on we all left hygiene behind, letting our beards grow and gradually picking up increasingly more scent.

The next day Don Koopmans and another hunter, Bob from Pennsylvania, joined us. Don was a very lean thirty-five years of age, but he looked forty-five. He had been a rodeo rider and had played semi-pro hockey. A bush pilot, he was extremely well educated in wilderness survival. He was in excellent condition and could walk for several days without becoming fatigued.

Don's van had at least one hole in the exhaust system. It was rather rickety, but it had a large rack on the top and easily accommodated everyone physically, except that the poor soul who rode behind the driver got gassed the whole way. Actually, we all were holding the windows open, gasping for air. I was fortunate that I had already arranged to sit up front and take pictures.

It took us about two and a half hours to drive to our guide Cody's house. He was a small, hyper man, probably five foot five, and he weighed at most 130 pounds. He was kind of a legend in his community. He had been a national bronco-busting rodeo champion in his youth, and he continued to participate in rodeo circles as a steer roper in his adult years. He carried with him a long Tegart family history of being hard and mountainous. Everyone in this little valley seemed to be named Tegart.

Beside the house was a large barn, better described as a packing shed. Upstairs Cody had all of his rodeo pictures, and places for the hunters to stay. He had no running water in that building, and there was an outhouse behind it. Downstairs was a large room where he did some taxidermy.

The front yard was gorgeous, and it looked out over the mountain ranges. Those views were tainted in the winter by as much as a foot of snow, which was usually manageable. This was not true in the mountains themselves. We were warned that if it started to snow up at Ralph Lake, we were going to have to leave immediately, because the snowflakes were sometimes as big as two inches across, and it was not unheard of to get four to eight inches of snowfall in just a few hours. It was quite possible to get snowed in, and the only way to get out then would be by an airlift.

Initially, when we were talking about the size of an elk, I didn't know what a five-by-five or a six-by-six was. I really thought they were talking about their size in feet, but I gradually learned about the number of points per an elk's side. The frontal tongs are those in the front of the horn that come forward over the animal's forehead. The cape is the skin that is over the shoulders and neck and comes up over the head and face.

Everybody was concerned that if we harvested our animals, we needed to retrieve an incisor tooth, as the game commission uses these to tell the age of the animals. We also learned that the "bugle teeth," or molars as we know them, should be removed from the animals simply because they had value. At the present time in Canada, a relatively unworn bugle tooth is worth fifty dollars, so everybody wanted to get the hind teeth from their animals to "add to their trophies."

The drive to the Palliser River base camp took us through Kootenay National Park. There was a river flowing through the bottom, and it was absolutely stunning. At the first mountain range we went through a narrow, extremely steep gorge. They had placed the road over the river, so we were actually driving on top of the river until we got through the canyon. We continued along the river through the marshlands until we got to a dirt road on which we travelled for about twenty miles. I was amazed that the road was smooth enough that we were able to drive about forty to forty-five miles an hour. It was a wide road, designed for logging and mining trucks to use while travelling through the national park.

Base camp had a two-storey log cabin with an addition on the back. There were bunk beds in the back room and sleeping quarters upstairs for the guides. There was an outbuilding with a wood stove and a bathtub where you could carry water, if you were desperate enough to have the room heated or to bathe. There was also a small cabin with a little wood stove and four beds in it. The next building was their tackle building. The upstairs quarters were where I would spend one night. There was nothing but plywood shelves to sleep on.

The Palliser territory is a large lease that takes in something like fifty square miles and covers a lot of mountain country. The Palliser River ran in front of our camp; you could see the bottom of the river very clearly, and it was easy to catch fish.

I met Grant Armstrong, a friendly cowboy with a bushy mustache who likely hadn't washed for about a week. Cody, his brother Larry, Grant and Don were really knowledgeable about handling horses and mules and packs. Grant helped load up the animals, and I held the mule. Her name was Jenny and her eyes were real pretty. She was two years old, and this was only her second trip. She was even-tempered, except while they were loading her with these tremendous loads and pushing and pulling.

We gathered around and got some instructions. For the first time, Cody looked at me and asked if I was in good shape. As false pride goes, I said that I was in average shape. That was a good one. I wondered if I would regret it. I was a little embarrassed that I wasn't in better shape, but being the oldest person in the party by at least ten years didn't help.

We proceeded up a beautiful valley. First it was kind of like a canyon, and then we went back and forth across the river several times. Parts of the valley were lush, with thick, dark-brown soil that the horses would churn up. There were tremendous rocks and trees on the trail, which we had to climb over. We would then get to moist valleys full of ferns and moss. As we headed up the slopes, the deciduous trees, mostly aspen and birch, became sparse. At the higher elevations the trees were predominately pine, spruce and tamarack.

As we continued up this valley, we rode horseback most of the way. We ran into areas that were long and linear, and covered in shale. I soon learned that this was due to avalanches, and you could see how the contour of the mountains really dictated where the avalanches would occur. Evidently, these could be quite violent. We saw one avalanche that, after having hit the bottom, went about four hundred yards up on the other side of the mountain. There was still, even in October, twenty feet of snow at that remote location.

The meadows were full and lush, with grass up to two or three feet tall. I learned that the large herds that are forced to the bottom land in the winter gradually thin out due to food shortage there. Then when the smaller survival herds migrate back up to the mountaintops in the summer, they have an overabundance of grass and foliage to feast on, more than they could ever eat.

It took us three and a half hours on horseback to go up this valley. I was given a horse called Freckles. She was a very nice, powerful horse, and fortunately very gentle, although extremely round backed. I was happy wherever we got the opportunity to get down and walk a little bit. The mountain before we got to camp was tremendous. It must have been a mile and a half walk uphill, with a lot of switchbacks, roots and rocks. We started leading the horses, but I got winded so badly that I eventually got back on the horse and she carried me over some of the roughest terrain. I was beginning to realize that this was not going to be a good week for my body.

At the top of the mountain there was some fencing to keep the animals from running back home. We went through a gate and down into a pasture area between the mountains, where Queen Mary Cabin overlooked a little creek, a tremendous rock bluff and the most gorgeous emerald-green lake.

The cabin was three stories tall and had a beautiful deck. It had a door that you could hardly open and shut because it was so big, with a handle made from moose antlers. There was a large table that we all sat around and told our stories. The beds were plywood and the benches were hard. There was nothing soft to sit on anywhere, so we gradually became accustomed to sitting on rocks, the ground, plywood or cut logs. The cabin had some snow damage that had caused the house to shift a little bit, which broke one of the upper beams. Because of this they had a chain going across from the main support beam on the roof on the third deck to the other one to support it, and then they had that chain attached to a come-along, which was attached to a tree on the side of the mountain behind the building. As the guides went to bed at night and told their stories and wiggled around, you could feel the building shift.

I didn't know it at that time, but the guides were all trying to size us up. Their ideal is a track star who can run a hundred miles and keep up with them, as they hunt by covering tremendous territory, not necessarily by using a great deal of hunting skill. They all lived life on the edge. The other thing the guides looked for was someone carrying a Skoal tobacco can, because they knew that they could get in his Skoal during their trip.

Cody's nephew Doug was our camp cook. He was thin and lean and earned his living off-season with guided backpacking and river rafting tours. He was an excellent cook and a very nice youngster. But he was more interested in picking up rocks and being a naturalist. He was what the other guides called a "tree hugger," and they semi-affectionately referred to him as Alfalfa Sprout. He had a lot of liberal ideals and was interesting to talk to. Camp talk was rather "colourful" at times.

The conversations were very interesting. Everyone was fairly educated in world events. There were a lot of economic questions and comparisons between Canada and the United States, and there were also a great number of jokes of varying degrees of colour. I found that our guides and the organizers of our trip lived with a tremendous amount of reckless abandon, climbing cliffs and taking risks.

One morning Alfalfa Sprout finished his cooking and decided that he was going to be my guide. We climbed straight up a shale cliff and looked out over the most gorgeous rim into another valley. This was also the kick-off point to go to Ralph Lake. It half killed you just to get to that point where you began the trip. Then we swung down underneath a rock ledge and travelled across the edge of a mountain above the shale on an elk trail for about two miles. We then went down into the valley through a glacial slide and across the marshy valley up into a little notch, where I was shocked at the number of tracks and the amount of sign that I saw.

That was the first place I saw what they called a "fool's hen," also known as a spruce grouse. The fool hen just simply sat there while Alfalfa Sprout took a rock and threw it at it a couple of times. We got within ten feet of it and it still wouldn't fly, and finally he hit it in the head and killed it. We would have fool-hen gravy several times during our trip.

My feet were on fire and I knew they were all blistered, but Alfalfa Sprout was intent on climbing this mountain. We went through the heavy growth and up over a couple of small cliffs and finally got to the top. The view was incredible, and we were so high, it looked like we were almost in the clouds. I called this spot the "mole hill." One could see numerous slides, and it was the apex of listening to all the elk calls. We could identify over eight major elk that evening.

When we got back to camp, J.D. and Don had finished their mountain goat hunt. JD had already shot his five-by-four elk and a reasonable goat of about nine inches. I kept thinking, *My god, I'm out of shape. These guys want to run, run, run to get the animals. I'm going to be here all week, just trashing my body.*

I was sure I would be the last of the group to get anything, but I made up my mind that I was going to do my very best. I did share my opinion with Grant that it seemed to me Alfalfa Sprout wasn't terribly interested in hunting. From then on Grant was my guide. Grant and I gradually developed a strong relationship. I think we thoroughly enjoyed each other's personalities, and I enjoyed learning about his lifestyle. Each day I got stronger, and while I could never outdo Grant, I could push him a little bit toward the end.

Grant wore a big white hat and had a big, heavy, relatively ill-kept mustache that hung down over his lip. He was a true cowboy, and like Cody and many of the others, he always had his big rodeo belt buckle on. His family owned an eighteen-hundred-acre farm in Alberta. His wife was an avid horsewoman and was still barrel racing and calf roping. He flew airplanes, played hockey and lived life on the edge. At times he showed a great deal of wilderness skill, yet I found him to be very well educated and sophisticated.

On the same day that I climbed the little mountain with Alfalfa Sprout, Louie Kugler and Mark, his guide, had a nice hunt. They were off to a very good start and got within a couple of hundred feet of an elk. Louie wasn't prepared when the elk suddenly appeared and charged past him. He didn't get off a shot because the whole episode took him by surprise. This was rather unfortunate, because this was the best chance Louie would get. Louie and Mark hunted very diligently throughout the trip and probably put more physical energy into hunting than any other members.

Mark was a quiet, thin boy, about five foot six, who also sported a rodeo belt buckle. He was supposed to be an excellent hockey player. His ability to climb mountains on the run exceeded anyone in the group. He was the nearest thing to a mountain goat, and he literally could climb mountains and not be winded. Louie and Mark got along very well, and Louie was very pleased with his trip.

I began to hunt with Grant, and that was the apex of my trip. We packed our horses and rode out of camp, through the notch and then down the mountain we had climbed to get into camp. We went by a creek, tied up our horses and Grant and I started to walk in. My feet were tender, but I was sucking it up. We were beside a mountain stream that was making so much noise we could hardly talk. It was very wet and mossy and loaded with elk wallows. We could see good fresh signs, and we began to get a little fever. We went in a couple hundred yards and Grant said he wanted to go back because he wasn't sure he'd tied up the horses well enough. I said I would stay up there, and I sat down beside a big log. I watched very carefully, because I was looking over a slide and thought there might be some possibility of an animal walking out. Soon, down came a beautiful elk cow. She didn't see me and walked to within fifteen feet of me. As she caught wind of me, her ears folded back, her head went into the air and she turned and walked away.

When Grant came back and I told him about the cow, he said, "Usually when you get into cows you can't get the bull." We went a couple hundred yards farther along the stream and walked up on a second cow. This cow wasn't startled and moved a short distance away. Grant was convinced we weren't going to get anything, so we decided to head back out to another location. Before heading back, Grant suggested that we try to bugle a little bit. He bugled a couple times and we had two answers.

Grant asked, "You want to try?"

I said, "Absolutely! I wasted my feet yesterday, so I'm going for this one." We started up through the thick brush, trying to make as little noise as possible. We would bugle, and the bulls would answer back. It must have taken us two hours to get halfway up the mountain. I was gradually getting a little stronger, and beginning to get fairly apt at walking across logs without killing myself or breaking my leg.

We kept climbing and bugling. Grant was giving the cow calls under his arm. We were gradually positioning ourselves between the big bull elk and his cows. Suddenly we heard this call that was different from any of the others. It sounded as if this animal was in the same room with us. I looked at Grant, and he looked at me and said, "Oh shit!" and we just stood still.

I was downhill of Grant and on an incline of probably sixty degrees. I was standing behind some fallen logs, and the height was just proper for me to stand and lay my gun on them. The bull bugled directly above us, but we couldn't see anything. We also couldn't hear a thing, so I got my gun up and waited for the animal. I thought he would come straight to me, but instead he came in from my right and snapped a twig. That was enough to allow me to turn in that hole and face him, so that neither Grant nor I had to move. If we could have moved at that point, I think we would have lost our animal.

He looked right at us, and all I could see was his eyes, his forehead and one horn. I could see it was a large horn and knew I was going to take him if I got the opportunity. We knew he was moving behind the brush, and even though he was less than twenty-five feet from us, we couldn't see him. There was a small break in the brush, and I could see that was where he was going. I had my scope up to six power, which was worthless, so I just followed him with the barrel of the gun until he stepped into this little opening. I saw his chest as it came in, and knowing right where his heart was, I pulled the trigger.

That elk turned completely upside down and became wedged between a log and a stump. I looked at Grant and I told him I could kiss him. He was jubilant, and we just sat there with our mouths hanging open. The animal was kicking a little and Grant told me to shoot it again just in case it tried to get up. We were both amazed because this was a tremendous bull elk with a massive rack. I was more awed by his overall size at that moment than his rack.

Grant and I were jumping around like little boys, looking at those horns. We started to remove the cape, and I bitched at Grant because the horns were so big that they kept getting in our way. It was a little difficult because the animal was wedged in and he was so heavy, but we finally removed the cape and salvaged the horns and the tenderloin.

Because we were in such a remote area with all this deadfall, and with the horses over two miles away, I didn't see how we were going to get any of the meat out other than the tenderloins, head and cape, as there were grizzly bears around. Grant and I took turns pulling this large animal downhill over all the windfalls. We worked another half a day just to get the hindquarters, horns, tenderloin, my gun and the cape about a quarter of the way down to the creek.

We were fortunate to run into an elk trail, and we decided that we would gamble and leave our trophies in that location, hoping that a bear wouldn't come around before we could return with the horses. We walked out with the cape and the antlers. We found the horses and led them back up, making our own trail. We had to ford a fast-moving creek but did so without any difficulty. We made it to a tree I had marked at the edge of the glacier. You couldn't even see where the elk trail was on the glacial side, and we just had to duck through the pine until we hit it. As we got to our animal, the horses got really spooky from the smell of blood. They could see that there was something there, and Grant became very concerned that there might be a bear in the vicinity. Fortunately, there wasn't.

The hindquarters were so heavy that Grant and I couldn't lift them onto the horse. We tried to make a lean-to against the saddle with a big tree, but the horse was skittish and moved away a couple of times. Finally, we took an axe and we split the spine and pelvis open and skinned the quarter so that the hide made a saddle. I talked Grant into putting a stick in the middle and then we had something good we could lift by. The two of us were able to lift this high enough to place a quarter on each side of the horse, with the elk rump tied over the saddle with a notch for the saddle horn to go through. This was all the securing needed, and it rode on that horse very securely the rest of the way to camp.

It was now about four o'clock, and it had been about five hours since we shot the animal. We tied the elk horns on the other horse and began the walk home. This was an interesting ordeal for someone whose feet were so tender, but I simply had to make up my mind that we were going to keep going. We had to walk back up the mountain in order to get back to camp. Once at the top we just took it easy and slid back into camp at dusk.

Everybody was aghast at the size of the horns, running out and measuring this and measuring that. While not official, the four guides scored them as being somewhere between 314 and 320. It was a perfect six-by-six, with only one horn an inch shorter than the others. They were eight inches at the base, extremely heavy and very dark in colour. It was a beautiful rack. We gave the camp cook the tenderloin. We were exhausted, so we didn't do any more work on the cape that night. We had a good meal and went to bed. I felt a great deal of relief.

The next day, I was ready for a rest. I was rather surprised at what I had been physically able to do the day before and a little proud of myself. We lazily took our time in the morning, and Grant began to finish off my cape. In the afternoon Grant and Alfalfa Sprout went looking for other elk, hoping they could help Louie get a kill. They wanted to get that done early in the week, so we could really enjoy ourselves. They spent three days hunting some wise old bull who would occasionally let them see him, but they never really got a shot, so Louie ended up without an elk. He had a tremendous adventure but left without a trophy.

That afternoon I was left in camp alone, and for the first time in years I had the idea that the world had slowed down enough to let me back on it. I could not believe the quiet solitude with only myself, the birds and a few other little animals. I went fishing. The lake was so prolific in small fish that I could not throw my fly out more than three times without catching a fish. I actually got tired of taking the little fish off. I found the deeper portions of the lake and was able to catch a lot of nice trout. I got about twenty-five trout before I quit.

The walk back from the lake was quiet, and I recalled how on the first night Grant and I had seen a porcupine alongside the lake. We had chased the porcupine, and when Grant got close he threw his hat up against it, and the hat was immediately filled with several hundred quills. I was happy it wasn't my hand or part of my body. I was also amazed that the porcupine, after having been chased, stopped only twenty feet from us and began to eat. I guess he thought we were full of those quills and wouldn't bother him anymore.

One day we decided to go back to Ralph Lake. We got to an outlook that had a view over the shale bank, and we looked down through the long valley, which must have had twenty slides on it. We worked our way along the top edge of the mountain, as we were heading about six ridges over to drop down into the large valley that housed Ralph Lake. It became obvious that this was an impressive climb and it was going to take everything I had to complete it.

We made it to the next shale bank, which overlooked some glacier ice, and spotted a herd of goats. We worked our way down the shale slope and descended gradually into a large basin to a beautiful lake. This was true wilderness country, because only four or five people came here each year. There was a little A-frame cabin, kind of like a tent with heavy plastic over logs with a wood stove. Alfalfa Sprout caught a twenty-one-inch trout in the lake, and everybody had a fillet that afternoon.

Across from the lake I went hunting one afternoon and saw another porcupine, coyote tracks, wolf tracks and bear tracks. Grant climbed to the top of the ridge where nobody but Don had gone before they referred to it as Don's Valley. Don had gotten a goat in that valley, but it was extremely steep and three valleys away from camp. At the top of that ridge there was a game trail, and Grant came back and remarked that the trail was freshly used and had a lot of elk sign on it.

We slept at that cabin that night, and we had a little experience in how to make a bed from spruce bows and how to sleep under a tree so we didn't freeze. I was very much aware of this from Boy Scout days and decided that I was going to sleep out in the open. I had found a nicely contoured place that was out of the wind. With my raincoat for a little windbreak for my face, I slept in my mummy bag that night, and I must admit that I was very comfortable. I was a little surprised at how much frost was on me the next morning, as the temperature must have gone down close to twenty Fahrenheit that night.

Grant and I decided to hunt on our way back, so we left Ralph's Lake earlier than the others. I was proud I was able to walk back over all that rough terrain; I really didn't have any difficulty until we got to the last shale bank before camp. Grant picked the wrong trail, and we went up probably the most dangerous and hazardous way that we could go. One slip and we would be another two or three thousand feet down the mountain lickety-split, with nothing to grab onto. It was extremely steep, well over a seventy-degree incline, but we kept going and made it alive. Grant later apologized to me for taking me over it.

About the second day of hunting, Grant took me to the top of another mountain, where we saw some mule deer as they ran away. There was a shortcut across a cliff with a four-inch ridge where you could walk, overlooking a fall of several hundred feet. I told Grant that wasn't my style, so we went the long way and walked the whole way around the top of the mountain into a big alpine meadow. That ridge was the only thing I refused to do on the whole hunt.

We began to pack to get ready to head home. I had gear strung out everywhere. My clothes were dirty, and I was ready to leave this tremendously beautiful environment. I rode the whole way back, which took two and a half hours as opposed to the three and a half hours coming in. It was downhill more than up, and the animals wanted to go home, so at times they would break into a trot. We ran into several groups of whitetail deer coming back.

We were very happy to get back to base camp. Grant brought his vehicle for us to load our gear, and J.D., Grant and I headed back to Cody's. I had been treated very well and rewarded Grant with a generous tip, so he was feeling kind of social and in no hurry to go home. Louie, Don and Alfalfa Sprout had stayed back to hunt.

We enjoyed catching up with everyone at Cody's house. Mike was there, and everybody was showing off their horns and telling stories. Cody had taken the Elk Federation president and a photographer out on a personal hunt, and he had shot a six-by-six. The photographer then got the bug and had gone in town and bought a licence. Cody got him out on a hunt, and he got a six-by-six. A man by the name of Jim Anderson, who hunted in the flats with Mike, had shot a six-by-six, a little longer in the beam than mine, but not as pretty, as it had one of its horns broken off on a major point. Mike had hunted with Cody's brother, Larry, and had gotten a five-by-five, with a smaller rack in height and width. The rack acquired by DJ was a five-by-four. It was a nice size and fairly wide.

The others had already had a chance to clean and shave up. Everybody was drinking beer. We got organized, and even though we were unshaven and smelly, we joined the others at a restaurant for supper.

The next morning we got up and had breakfast with Cody and Linda. We then proceeded over to the packing shed, where we all sat around comparing racks, taking photographs and packing the horns and capes for our trip home. That was all very special and relaxed, and the mountain view from Cody's front yard was gorgeous.

We decided that we would like to go to a motel in town to await the other hunters before we proceeded home the next day. At this point we kind of picked on Grant and suggested, "Hey, it would be awful nice if you drove us to town." I had the idea that town was only about thirty minutes away. Coming in, I had been so hyped about the scenery and taking pictures out the car window that I hadn't realized we had driven a considerably long distance. It was actually about an hour and forty-five minutes. I felt guilty that Grant took us back.

We had an uneventful trip from Cranbrook to the airport, with Cody showing up at the last minute with our meat. It became obvious on my trip home that I had nowhere to put all this meat I had brought with me, so without waking up my mother, I raided her freezer and packed it full. I guess parents never do get rid of their kids!

I think it's extremely interesting to go back and remember certain little things besides the general flow of the trip.

I didn't see any grizzly, but Mike got far too close to one that charged. Evidently, they are very plentiful and come out of the national park. As soon as a gun goes off, they have been seen to change direction immediately and head in the direction of the gun sound, anticipating a meal.

As we went about our mountain climbs, we often saw little holes in the ground. These were due to marmots, little animals like small prairie dogs. The animals often chose a large rock to put their burrow under. This is because bears would try to dig them out. At places it really looked like backhoes had been at work at the top of the mountains, where the bears had attempted to extract the marmots from their dens.

The wallows made by the elk were quite prolific. Evidently, the bull elk would take his horns and front hooves and plow the ground up. They would apparently get in there and make mud and splash around to put their scent there to mark their territory.

This trip can go down as a true adventure in my life. I don't know if this old body could go through it all again, but I'm sure glad we made it through that one.

THE GOAT HUNT

BY GARY WEATHERBY

I was raised in the Windermere Valley during 1950s and 1960s and had the privilege of going to school and working with many of the Tegarts. They were long-time residents of the Windermere Valley and were well respected by those who knew them; they were good, hard-working, honest people.

I left the valley and worked in Alberta for a number of years, and in 1975 I became an instructor at the Southern Alberta Institute of Technology. In the 1980s a fellow instructor commented that he had a student by the name of Garrett Tegart. I went to see Garrett, and it was the beginning of a friendship that still exists today.

One fall Garrett and I were talking about hunting, and he commented that he was going out into the East Kootenays to guide a hunter on a goat hunt. I knew of the area he was talking about but had never been there, as it was common courtesy, growing up in the valley, not to hunt in an outfitter's territory. Garrett and I talked about his upcoming trip. I mentioned that it would be easier if he had a camp helper to cook and look after the chores around camp, and the conversation ended with Garrett asking if I would like to go along.

Garrett and I loaded up my Dodge Ramcharger and went to the Calgary airport to pick up an American hunter who had booked a hunt with Garrett's brother, Cody. We proceeded out to the East Kootenays though Banff National Park and branched off down Settlers Road, which follows the Kootenay River. The road was familiar, as I had worked in the area for Welder Brothers when I was a teenager, setting chokers and working in the portable sawmill, which moved to different areas being logged. It brought back memories, because one of the people I set chokers for was Happy Tegart, a cousin of Garrett's. I had gone to school with Happy and his sister.

That evening we arrived at base camp, which was active with everyone getting organized for the trip into Queen Mary the next morning. If I remember correctly, we had mule deer chili for dinner. I remember Cody telling the hunters that there was no smoking allowed, and he was handing out snooze and chewing tobacco. He also said to check their rifles at base camp because once they left main base camp, there was no shooting, except at the game being hunted.

At this time, it appeared that Cody had taken over managing the territory from his father, Jim, and his Uncle Buster. Garrett's mother and father were there, and we talked about my father and the old days. It was an honour to visit with them; they were good people. Most of the hunters slept in the base camp house, and I slept in the Ramcharger. Garrett's mother and father had their truck and camper. With all the talking and everyone either getting to meet each other or talking about hunts from before, it was not an evening to get a good sleep.

The next morning was busy, getting horses saddled and mules packed for the trip into Queen Mary. As I watched the hunters, I thought, *there are going to be a bunch of sore people tomorrow.* I think riders and horses were selected by the rider's experience around horses. Some of the hunters, I am sure, had little exposure to horses and how to ride. The horses and mules were tailed, and I am sure they had made the trip many times before. I would estimate the trip to be about ten or twelve miles. The country was beautiful, and from time to time we could hear a bull elk bugle, as the rut was in full swing. We arrived at Queen Mary early in the afternoon, unsaddled the horses, unpacked the mule and put them in a corral. Tack was put away and pack boxes were unpacked. There were no roads here, so everything had to be packed in by horses or mules.

I had made a pair of aluminum pack boxes for Cody, but he looked at them in question; this was something new for him, and maybe he really didn't know what to think of them. I must ask someday what ever happened to them.

Queen Mary Lake interested me, because the fish were jumping, and I had brought my fly-fishing rod. The fish were small, ten to twelve inches, but the water was ice cold right off the glacier, and this means excellent-tasting fish. I was told they were rainbow trout, but I believed they were golden trout, which are native to high-altitude lakes in BC and look like rainbow trout except for the golden colour. They were easy to catch, as I doubt that few people bothered to fish for them.

The Queen Mary Camp was well organized and very picturesque, with the lake and Mount Queen Mary with its glacier in the background. The log house and the horses feeding painted a picture of such beauty that only by being there can one really appreciate it all. The camp had a camp cook who I thought did a great job. He baked fresh bread and put a good meal on the table. He was from the valley and had a pleasant personality. A camp cook is the first person up in the morning and the last to bed at night, so I have a lot of respect for them, as it's not an easy job. It must be noted that the cooking was done on a wood stove, and most people today would have little knowledge on how to start a fire in it, let alone cooking a decent meal and baking bread with one.

That night I slept in the hay shelter while the hunters and guides slept in the log house. I could hear the snoring from outside, and with me being a light sleeper, that was no place to get any sleep. I slept so soundly that it was daylight when I woke up. Garrett was up, and after a bite to eat, we started getting ready to go to Ralph Lake. The hunter, Garrett and I would be taking what we needed in our backpacks and on a pack mule. The climb out of Queen Mary to Ralph Lake is too steep for a horse. We had packed up a new mule that Cody had. He was a good-looking mule but had the confirmation of a riding mule. The mule couldn't make the steep climb, so the hunter and I continued to the top. I took Garrett's pack and Garrett took the mule back down and packed a small mule that had been packed a lot; I think her name was Mizz. Even for a seasoned pack mule, the climb was not easy, and the terrain was rough and steep up and down. A breast collar and britching were needed to try to keep the pack in place.

The elevation at Ralph Lake is in the seven-thousand-foot range, and with the fast rise in elevation, I had to take a break and let my body adjust for about half an hour and then all was good. As we topped the ridge before dropping down into Ralph Lake, we were treated to a spectacular view, with the mountain background and the blue-green lake along with the peace and tranquility of it all.

After unpacking the mule and tethering her out, we organized the small shelter, which had an airtight wood stove for heat and shelves for food. There were a few supplies, such as matches, salt and pepper and other miscellaneous items. The chimney from the stove went up a short distance and then out the back wall. When darkness settled in, the hunter and Garrett set up in the shelter while I slept outside. I had brought a five-star woods sleeping bag, and if anything I thought I might be too warm. Garrett had started a fire in the stove to cut the night chill, but as the air cooled, it started to drop, and with this the stove had more back pressure than it could push. Soon the Hunter and Garrett were standing outside, with the smoke from the stove pouring out the door. I never had much luck with a short chimney running horizontal. After a while the air stabilized, the stove died down and we went back to bed for a good night's sleep.

The next morning, early, I got a fire going, cooking outside over a fire pit and grating, with a flashlight and frying pan. The smell of bacon and eggs cooking over a campfire in the cool mountain air will give a person an appetite that is unbelievable. After breakfast the hunter and Garrett set out. I went down to the lake to get water to heat for washing dishes, and I noticed fish rising to take bugs on the lake's surface. After I put the pot of water on the fire to heat, I took out my fly rod and tied on a dry fly. I cast the fly onto the water and right away I had a bite, and to my surprise it was a nice-sized cutthroat trout, maybe

While hunting near Ralph Lake, some hunters also partook in fly-fishing. Using gathered stones and the grill from the fire pit, Gary Weatherby smoked these trout, which were quickly devoured by hungry returning hunters.

three pounds. For me, fly-fishing cutthroat trout is the very best. No matter how big they are, they seem to take a dry fly, which is my favourite form of fly-fishing. I cast again and this time the fish was even bigger.

When fishing alpine lakes, we must remember that reproduction is small and growth is slow, so it's important not to take more than you need to eat. I cleaned the fish, and after washing the dishes I gathered stones and built a stone smoker. With coals from the fire pit and a gathering of shrubs, I had my trout smoker ready. I used the grill from the fire pit for a grate to put the fish on and used a little seasoning. With a low heat I smoked the fish until the hunter and Garrett returned. They were hungry, and the smoked trout soon disappeared, along with whatever else I had cooked.

I don't remember, but I think it was the next day that the hunter shot his goat. I had told Garrett that they should bring back the loins and back straps. That afternoon they returned with the head and skin, as the hunter wanted a full mount, and the loins and back straps. The next day I cut the goat meat into strips about one-half-inch thick and seasoned them with allspice. I took a piece of wood, placed the meat on a flat rock and pounded the strips to a thickness of about a quarter of an inch. I prepared the smoker and smoked the goat meat all day. Garrett was busy fleshing the goat skin, skinning out the head, turning out the lips and ears and taking the knuckles out of the feet. If one hasn't done this or seen it first-hand, it is a lot of work, and then the hide must be salted to prevent it from spoiling till the taxidermist can work with it.

We were visiting and doing some camp chores when we heard a distant elk bugle. Garrett went to his pack, took out an elk bugle tube and gave a bugle, and almost immediately the elk replied. Garrett bugled again, and the bull elk appeared on the far side of the lake. He was a good bull, a mature six-by-six, and I thought there was probably a hunter or two at Queen Mary who would like to be where we were. Garrett bugled again, and the bull became very aggressive and wanted to challenge. After about fifteen minutes, he disappeared. That evening I caught two more fish and let them smoke during the night. The hunter seemed to enjoy the fish, and he carried a bag of goat jerky with him.

The next morning we broke camp and started back to Queen Mary. We were partway back when we met up with another hunting party who were doing a stalk on a goat. Goats can be cautious. If they become nervous, they will go for high ground, and they can climb where a person would think it was impossible to climb. Where a sheep has difficulty, a goat will climb with ease. The goats had noticed us and were starting to climb. The guide told the hunter that he didn't think they could get closer without the goats climbing to where they couldn't be retrieved if shot. The hunter said he would take the shot from where we were. I thought it was a long shot from where we stood. I would estimate it was close to five hundred yards and uphill. The hunter had a 7mm Magnum rifle, and he took a rest and made the shot. He was relaxed and showed he was very capable, and the shot was good.

The hunter, Garrett and I continued back to Queen Mary Camp. The sky was clear and the air was clean, as only it can be when human activities have not polluted everything they touch. It was something I wish everyone could experience, but then that would result in pollution. Humans do not live with nature; they adjust everything to be as they want it to be.

At Queen Mary we unpacked, and Garrett checked out the cape and hide. The hunter was relaxing, and at the camp cook's request, I went down to the lake and caught some fish, providing a nice change for the hunters and guides in camp. We had been having smoked fish, smoked goat meat and canned meat at Ralph Lake, so our diet had more variety than they'd had at Queen Mary.

The next morning we saddled horses and started back to main camp by the Kootenay River. I preferred to walk that morning, as the sun was shining, the sky was blue, the air had a beautiful fall smell and I wanted to enjoy as much as I could. The hunter walked with me, enjoying it as much or maybe even more than I did. Garrett was riding and bringing the other two horses. I envied Garrett and his family, who had been doing this for many, many years and had shared it with many others in the past. It is a lot of work, but to be able to live and experience this lifestyle is something I dream of, which I know most cannot understand.

We arrived in base camp, loaded Garrett's and my things in the Ramcharger, said our farewells and started back to Calgary.

Garrett and I keep in touch and reminisce about the hunt into Ralph Lake sometimes. The weather was perfect, the country was spectacular, the company was the best, and it is one of my fondest memories. I said to Garrett that he and I should make a trip down memory lane, and he commented that the area is now open to hikers and backpackers, and with government intervention, it is not the same. So best I keep the memories of almost thirty years ago.

I want to thank Garrett and Cody for letting me experience a part of their life and visit paradise with them.

WHO WAS THAT HUNTER? by Garrett Tegart

Two weeks prior to going guiding for Cody in September 1994, while breaking a young stud colt, I broke my eye socket and had to have a metal plate put in my head. Cody phoned and asked if I was still coming to guide. I told him yes. I loaded my horses and picked up a hunter, who was from California, at the Calgary airport. He introduced himself as Kevin, and he seemed nice enough.

We headed to the Palliser. Around Canmore it started to snow, and we saw a shitload of elk. Going through Banff and Kootenay National Parks, we saw a lot more elk along the road. After a four-hour drive, we arrived at Fisher Creek Cabin. The only man there was the old caretaker who looked after Cody's cabins.

The next morning, before the break of day, we hiked above Fisher Creek to see if we could find a goat. Along the way, Kevin kept asking, "What is that terrible smell?" I told him it was either bear or sasquatch. We stopped for lunch, and I pulled out the sandwiches from my backpack to discover they were soggy and stank of the scent the hunter had been complaining about. I realized then that I had not taken my trapping scents out of my backpack, and the bottles had broken. Needless to say, we went hungry that day, and I think Kevin was a little less than impressed. However, we hiked on and spotted a lone billy up on a scree slide between two rock bluffs. We climbed to where Kevin had a good clear shot, and he downed him with one shot. We skinned him out, headed back to camp for the night and enjoyed a good meal. After all, we were a little hungry for some reason, but I think Kevin got over it as he had early success.

The next day we saddled up and headed to Queen Mary Camp, where we spent the night in the cabin. Kevin marvelled at the spectacular scenery, but then again, everyone does. We had no luck spotting an elk going there or on the way back to Fisher Creek.

The next day we headed up Sun Dog Creek. On the way up, Kevin and his horse fell into a bog hole, filling the barrel of his gun with mud. I pulled them out and we proceeded up the trail, where we stopped and sat on a log while we glassed the slides. We spotted a large herd of elk above us on the next ridge, but they were impossible to get to, so we headed back to camp just before dark, as it began raining and then snowing. As we crossed the Palliser, my horse reached out to grab a mouthful of grass, lost his balance and I ended up in the river. After a hard trot, we made it back to Fisher Creek Cabin, cold and wet. So far, I had starved Kevin and dumped him in a mudhole. I was thinking my tip might be in jeopardy.

At Fisher Cabin Darryl McLean, another guide, and his hunter had arrived. We enjoyed a few drinks that night. The next day Darryl and his hunter were going to Tipperary, so we packed up and headed out with them. We left them at Joffre Creek, and I took my hunter and a pack string up to the Top of the World, where we found sign but no elk.

We spent a cold night before heading out to Tipperary Cabin the next day. Linda was in camp, but all the boys were gone, so we rode up to Bridge Lake, which is a long ride. I still did not know Kevin very well, but he was game to hunt, and that was all that counted. Back at camp Linda said the guides and hunters were all up at Grizzly Ridge, so we headed up that way. The horses and the poor hunter were damn tired by the time we arrived. We met Billy McKay, Texas Tim, Cody and Darryl just as it was getting dark.

I had the use of only one eye, as my face had started to swell, so Cody made me stay in camp the next day, and he took my hunter and horses up Squaw Creek. Gordon Burns arrived at Tipperary Cabin that afternoon. I told him Cody was taking my place, as my eye had swollen closed, and that he had my horses. That night, when the boys met Kevin, they told me who he was. He was Kevin Bacon, the movie star. I guess I had missed his movies.

The next morning Cody spotted a herd of elk above the Three Waterfalls, not too far from Tipperary while getting water. Kevin and I headed up after them, and we spotted a nice six-point bull. We snuck up to about two hundred yards, and Kevin took his shot. The elk went down, and I made him shoot again just to make sure, as he had only brought three shells with him. I'm not sure why he only brought three shells. I think he may have been upset that I made him eat breakfast before we headed out that morning, as I thought it might be a long day.

Anyway, his elk was down and he was happy, so I gave him my axe and knife to cape the elk while I went back to camp to get mules to pack it out. I told him to be careful, as there was a grizzly up there and he had only one shell left. I met Cody on the way back to Kevin, so he came along to help. On the way back, we heard a ruckus. It was Kevin heading down the trail, hell bent for leather with the whole neck and horns on his back. He thought he'd seen a grizzly. That night, we all had a good laugh.

The next day we all packed up to head home, and Kevin asked if I was taking him back to Calgary. I told him that Texas Tim would be taking him. So, they headed to the airport in Tim's old truck, with two mules, an elk head, a goat and a bottle of whiskey. Kevin wrote me later and said that was "one hell of an adventure" and that he enjoyed the fact that I never really knew who he was and had treated him like a regular guy. I got a nice tip, and he got his game. In my mind, I was just another guide and he was just another hunter.

THE BACK SIDE OF BEAR CREEK by Randy Atwood

One day Cody, John Adams and I were cutting trail on the back side of Bear Creek. We would tie the horses, cut a hundred yards or so, then go fetch them and start cutting again. We came to a washout creek with no water in it. The creek bank was about nine feet deep, and the trail came really close to the edge. The creek bottom was strewn with boulders the size of your kitchen table.

At a five-inch birch tree that we should have cut but didn't, the trail panned away from the wash. We went back to bring up the horses, and Cody was riding his and leading a pack horse. Cody's horse made it by the birch, but the pack horse, whose name was Big Red, was looking at the creek bottom and forgot about his pack boxes sticking out the side. A pack box struck the tree, which spun his ass end around, and he ended up falling upside down into the wash. We all swore a bit in unison.

The only thing that saved the horse's life were the pack boxes, but he ended up wedged tightly between two boulders and was thrashing about. Cody and I quickly climbed down into the wash using two halter shanks. We held his front hooves to keep from getting kicked, and I reached down and cut the latigo and the lash rope at the cinch. Cody and I both pulled on his halter shank but couldn't get him upright. Big John threw down one end of a lash rope, and I tied it to his shank. We all leaned into it and pulled Red up on his feet.

The only gravel in the wash was where he was standing, close to the cutbank in an area about five feet square. Now we realized there was no way to go up or down the creek bed, because the boulders were too big and there was nowhere to place his step. Red was looking at Cody as if to say, "Well, how are we getting out of this mess?" He was bleeding from his head where he had smashed it on the rocks and had a gash on his flank from the pack box.

Cody and I weighed our options, and there were only two we could think of. One was to head back to town to get a pick and shovel and dig a trench up the wall, and the other did not have a happy ending for Red and involved an ounce of lead.

What happened next was the most amazing sight I have ever seen. Red knew he was in trouble and we weren't going to be much help. He could hear his buddies neighing up top, and he called back to them. He looked up at the top of the bank, then up and down the wash a couple of times, surveying his options. Then he looked back at Cody and me. His look said, "If you two aren't going to help me, then I'll do it myself." Red took one more look at the top of the bank, squatted down on all fours and catapulted himself for the top. His front hooves caught the top of the bank, with his back hooves scratching for traction, and then *bam*, he was up and standing on the trail.

We all stood there, amazed. Red was vibrating and broke into a sweat, most likely from an adrenalin high or from shock setting in. It took a half hour or so for us to get the rigging up and to fix the latigo. When we looked at Red, he was with his buddies, munching on grass and buckbrush. Cody said, "He looks fine to me, so never say 'whoa' in a mudhole." We packed him up and headed up the trail.

CODY AND THE WARDEN by Bob Jamieson

Years back Cody got his geography a bit mixed up and killed a goat just inside Banff National Park. He was a bad boy. So he was not popular in the offices of Parks Canada.

The next summer he had a big group of people from Calgary who wanted to go into Tipperary Cabin. Rather than drive all the way around to the Palliser, they asked Cody to pick them up in the Spray River Valley above Canmore. That way, they could ride up through the Upper Spray River Valley, in Banff Park, over Palliser Pass and go down to the cabin in the Palliser. Cody asked for a permit to take the party through the park and was turned down. So, Cody being Cody, he did it anyway. He took the horses over from the Palliser and down the Spray to the end of the road just outside the park. They mounted up and rode up and over Palliser Pass and had a great trip. Meanwhile, Parks Canada had heard about the horses going through.

On the way back out, Cody was leading the string down the Spray when he saw a warden, on horseback, with a pack horse, coming up the trail. The warden stopped Cody and asked, "Have you seen Cody Tegart?"

Cody said, "That son of a bitch! He is right up the trail. Go get him!" The warden charged up the trail, and Cody continued on his way. The guests departed, and Cody spent the night at the trailhead. The next morning, he was running his bunch of about twenty head up the trail in front of him. Halfway up the Spray River meadows, who does he see coming back down the trail but the warden, who ran smack into Cody's bunch of loose horses. His horse wanted to go with the bunch and started dancing around, and the warden got bucked off. As Cody went by, he tipped his hat to the warden, who was lying in the grass and trying to hang onto his horse's reins, and asked, polite as hell, "So, did you catch the son of a bitch?"

AN OFFER I COULDN'T REFUSE

Sal and Armand, from New Jersey, somehow got my phone number and gave me a call. Sal informed me right away that if I guided him and his buddy Armand at the same camp, he would book me on the spot. Now these two characters joked that they were Mafia and both talked like the guys in the movies. Sal told me some pretty exciting stories during the hunt. Armand was a hairdresser with his own shop in downtown New Jersey, where the boys would meet on occasion. Sal was a bad shot with good luck, and Armand was a good shot with bad luck.

Bill McKay was guiding for me at the time, and Texas Tim was wrangling. I also had hunters and guides at Queen Mary Camp and a couple more hunters and guides at Tipperary with me. These guys were on my second hunt, so I knew where most of the good billies were, and Sal and Armand had combo goat, elk and deer tags.

After a good night's rest at Tipperary Camp, the five of us headed for Harry's Basin on the way to Bridge Lake. This basin was named after a great hunter from Virginia who had lost an arm and a leg in a hydro accident. I had spotted two big billies on the first hunt there and was hoping they hadn't moved. After a very tough climb up to the rim, with Sal and Armand hanging on to their horses' tails for dear life, we arrived in Harry's Basin. I had brought two mules, expecting to also get an elk, as it was a hot spot where we'd had bulls bugling during the last trip. The grizzlies were very bad in this area, and usually an elk carcass wouldn't last the night. We tied up the animals and walked the last way into the basin. Sure enough, on a ledge about two hundred yards away was billy number one, just lying down, chewing his cud.

Now, Sal weighed in at about 250 pounds and Armand about 130, so I decided the only fair way this goat hunt was going to go was to flip a coin. We hadn't spotted the other billy yet, so as I got ready to flip the coin, I was thinking, *If Armand gets it and Sal has to do any climbing, its going to be hard*. Sure enough, Armand won. We snuck to a nearby boulder about shoulder height, and Armand let loose with a shot. The billy was already lying down, so he just laid his head down and didn't move.

We all watched for a while, hoping the other billy would show himself after the shot, but nothing happened. As Bill and Tim started to climb up to the billy, I was looking around for the other one when down the mountain, they came running. They had spotted the other billy farther into the basin, lying on a ledge, chewing his cud. We all climbed up there, and it was Sal's turn. This goat was about three hundred yards up on the rock face above the scree slide, and we had no way of getting closer. We picked out the best boulder to shoot from, and Sal shot and missed. The goat jumped up and climbed straight up until he couldn't get any higher. I told Tim to drop some rocks on his head with his rifle, and then maybe he would come down. Sal didn't want to shoot him where he was at, in case he broke his horns during the fall. I honestly didn't think he could hit him anyway. Bill and I climbed up beside him and threw rocks to try to get him to move, but all he would do was stamp his front feet at us.

We finally gave up, and I told Bill and Tim to go skin the other billy while Sal and I watched this guy. As we started down off the mountain, the goat came down too. I'm guessing he wanted the hell out of there, because he had been peppered by Tim's bullets dropping on him and us throwing rocks at him. Every time we stopped to see if he would come into range, he stopped, so we proceeded on down. As soon as the goat reached the top of the scree, he headed toward his dead buddy. We set Sal back up again and he started blazing away. He soon ran out of shells, and Tim raced to the horses for more. Reloaded, he started again. Suddenly the goat swapped ends. Sal reloaded and finally finished it off.

With the goat down, we stopped for lunch, then Bill and Tim went over and skinned and quartered Armand's goat while I did Sal's. When we were done, Bill and Tim took the hunters on to Bridge Lake to look for elk. I headed back to camp with my mules to finish turning the goats' heads and feet, then I would flesh and salt the hides. When I reached the top of the bluffs above camp, I got off to lead the mules down the steep and slippery trail. As I took in the view of the cabin far below, with horses and mules grazing away in the meadow behind the camp, I noticed smoke coming from the chimney and heard the tinkle of bells worn by the horses. I heard an elk bugle, so I grabbed my bugle and answered. He replied, and I knew he was across the river from the cabin. I went on into camp, where my wife, Linda, was getting supper ready.

The other guides and the hunters didn't return until about a half hour before dark. I told Bill and Tim to leave the hunters' horses saddled and the rifles in the scabbards. I explained that a bull had bugled across the river on the slide and that he might still be there. I don't think they believed me, and Sal and Armand had already put their slippers on and poured a drink of bourbon.

I said, "The first guy out the door gets to go after the bull if he bugles." Sure enough, a couple minutes later, he bugled, and everyone heard it. The scramble was on, and Sal was the first one out the door. Cinches were tightened, and Bill hoisted Sal onto Poncho while I grabbed his halter shank, dallied it to my horn, and we were off in a flash. We hit the river at a trot, as we were running out of daylight fast. Up the trail we went and tied up at the bottom of the slide. There was a big boulder, just the right height for shooting from, and we reached it. I spotted the bull at the top of the slide about four hundred yards up. As I put my spotting scope on him, Sal asked how big he was. It was so dark I couldn't count the tines. My reply was that he was high and wide. *Boom!* I almost crapped my drawers as I saw the bull jump up and start running down the slide. He angled off across the slide at about three hundred yards and into a gully.

I knew I might never find him on foot, so I raced back to my mule, Jake. I told Sal to stay were he was until I knew what was going on. Jake and I headed up the rough, rocky, buck-brush-covered slide as fast as possible. I just got to where the bull left the slide when I heard his last exhale. I tied up Jake and pulled my flashlight from my belt pouch. Whew! It was a big six point, I figured about 330 points or more in Boone and Crockett scoring. He was piled up with his legs underneath him and couldn't be rolled over in the bottom of the gully. I got my axe off Jake and proceeded to cut off the side of the rib cage to get the guts out. The weather was very warm, so this was crucial.

As I was struggling to do this, Jake brayed, and a mule brayed back. Suddenly, Ralph Stewart appeared. He had been guiding Thurman Hensley, and they already had their elk, so he was coming into camp to join us. He heard the shot as they were coming up the gravel bar, so he sent Thurman on in with their pack string and came and found me in the dark. I was glad to see him, as I needed the help.

We were working away when the mules suddenly started fussing. *Crash, bang!* Here came Sal in his bedroom slippers! How in the hell he got up the slide in them was something else.

He asked, "What did I get?"

Ralph answered, "A spike." You could hear the wind go out of him like the dying bull. Ralph said, "See, a spike here and here and here," as he shone the light over the antlers. Now we had us a very happy hunter. He had shot and missed many times on a goat that same morning that was a whole lot closer than this bull in the dark. Now if this wasn't luck, then what was it?

We saw grizzly almost every day, and when the trip was over, Sal said he wanted the spring grizz hunt. Armand didn't get an elk, but he also wanted to come back for grizz.

The following spring arrived, and I picked up Sal and Armand at the Cranbrook airport. I had arranged that Armand was to hunt with my neighbouring guide outfitter, Chuck Christensen, just north of my territory. When I dropped Armand off at the old Frank Richter place (later known as Nipika), which was to be their base, Chuck and his son Mike met me there. I told Chuck there were fresh grizz tracks in the driveway. We all went and looked at them and commented that it was a very big bear.

I said, "You will probably get him in the next day or two." I should have remembered Armand's luck from the fall before compared to Sal's.

Sal and I headed for Fisher Creek. All along the way, the grizz tracks would appear on the road for a bit, travelling in the same direction we were. The road had just enough traffic on it to make dust for easy tracking. I stopped and checked the tracks and said to Sal, "They're very fresh, as there is no morning dew in them." Sure enough, we crossed the Palliser bridge, and as we rounded the corner, the bear was running up the road ahead of us. As soon as he heard the truck, he ran into the timber and we lost him. All we could do was go to base camp and hope for the best in the morning. Without bait, which had been banned years ago, or locating a favourite feeding area, finding a grizzly was extremely unpredictable.

One previous spring I had picked up a grizzly track coming over the pass from the north fork of the White River. It had snowed a couple inches the night before, and the tracks were fresh. The hunter and I drove as far as we could, following the tracks to the corral at the end of the Palliser road. The bear never left the road. We decided to grab the horses and some gear and follow him, as he had turned on to the pack trail at the corral. We continued on to Tipperary Cabin, and the only time he left the trail was to avoid the cabin by about a hundred yards. Who knows why he did this. We unpacked the pack horses, tied them up and continued following his tracks above the cabin. He had doubled back to the pack trail, which now had about two to three feet of snow on it. We continued to follow him until we reached the confluence of the Palliser River and Leroy Creek, where the snow got to be too deep for the horses. We tied up and followed on foot, sinking almost a foot in the spring-settled snow, about the same as the bear. He turned and started up the pack trail at Leroy Creek, heading toward the North Kananaskis Pass. This valley had beautiful, south-facing open slides in it, which I knew had slid earlier and would be green.

I was sure the bear would slow up to feed. It was very tough going, but the hunter was in excellent shape. As we approached the first green slide, I spotted what looked like the grizzly's shoulder hump in a small swale. We approached carefully, watching the wind, which was blowing toward him. When we got within fifty yards, I whispered to the hunter, "Let's stand up and shoot." He was ready, and as we stood up, in full view was a big old porcupine, not our grizzly. After that disappointment, I looked on up the valley with my spotting scope, and plain as day, there were the tracks of mister grizzly, crossing the pass to Alberta. They travel great distances in the spring, looking for a mate.

Back to Sal. The next morning, we headed for the Little Elk River. I started out earlier than normal, knowing a bear was in the area, plus there could be resident hunters about to head there. Gordon Burns, another guide, was in camp waiting for a black-bear hunter, who would be arriving in Cranbrook in a few days.

I suggested that Gordon take the black-bear hunter into a good area at the mouth of the Little Elk after I had about a

Sal, a hunter from New Jersey (right), and Darryl McLean (left) with an eight-foot grizzly.

half-hour head start. Sal, the guide and I drove straight up the Little Elk to a lookout point about three-quarters of the way up. This was a great spot to see the slides across the valley and some old logging in the bottom. I could see with my naked eye that there was a big boar and a sow on the slide. They were feeding very close together, so I knew she was in season. We watched them for a while, so I could figure out what to do, when suddenly, the big boar stood on his hind legs. About then, I heard Gordon's diesel truck start up the Little Elk road. The bear listened for a minute or two, then started for the timber above the logging, with the sow in hot pursuit.

I said to Sal and the guide, Doug, "See that high elk trail on the centre slide? We have to be on that trail north of the bears by four o'clock. They'll hole up in the timber for the day and do some breeding, then head north to feed. That's where we will intercept them."

Away we went back down the valley in the truck, and back up the bottom to where the bear had left. This was the end of the road, so now we started climbing up and north of where I figured the bear had holed up. Sal was a big man and sorely out of shape, so I would pull him up the steep spots while Doug packed our two rifles. We would swap chores when one of us got winded. This was a hell of a pile of work, and Sal didn't think he could make it.

I said, "Sal, you have no choice. Get your ass in gear or I'll tell your Mafia buddies how you missed the goat." Well, that got his goat and he had a little more try. Huffing and puffing, we arrived on the north side of a draw on the elk trail at five minutes to four. I sat Sal down with his loaded rifle, safety off, with the guide on one side of him and me on the other.

As I put a shell in the barrel of my rifle, safety off, Doug said to me, "I sure feel naked; there's not even a tree to climb, and those bears are going to come out across the draw at sixty yards."

I said, "Trust Sal. He shot his big bull elk last fall at four hundred yards in the dark. He's a damn fine shot."

At exactly four o'clock, the alders started shaking across the draw. I whispered to Sal, "The sow will be first, and she'll stop and look around when she's in the open. When she's happy the coast is clear, she'll continue down the trail and hopefully turn up the slide to feed. The boar will do the same, but don't shoot him until he starts down into the draw, then shoot him between the shoulder blades. I will keep track of the sow in case she charges."

Although we were in the open, the wind was blowing in our favour. I had also said not to move unless something went wrong. Well, the sow stepped out, looked around and started down the trail, followed by the boar. As soon as he started down the draw, *boom!* He died so fast, he just fell on his stomach.

I whispered loudly, “Don't move.” I held my crosshairs on the shoulder of the sow. She looked right at us, then looked back at the boar. She probably stood there four or five minutes, and my arms were getting tired. Finally, she started feeding up the slide, and every few minutes she would look back at the boar. I eased my rifle down slowly to give my arms a break.

Sal said quietly, “What do we do? Wow that was exciting!”

I replied, “Damn, you're a good shot, but we can't move yet. If she sees us, she might charge. She's not far enough away yet.”

We waited for about an hour, and when I felt she was far enough away, about two hundred yards, I told Doug to go grab the boar and try to drag him down the draw till she couldn't see him. I told Sal to stay put, but to be ready in case she charged. Doug eased over to the carcass slowly and was able to roll the bear down the mountain, out of sight of the sow. With this accomplished, Sal and I eased down until we were out of view of the sow. The wind was in our favour, and while one of us was always on guard with a loaded rifle, safety off, we took turns taking pictures.

Sal watched for the sow as Doug and I started skinning. This didn't take long, as we left the head and feet with the hide, which I would finish in camp. We headed down the mountain, happy as hell with a grizzly kill on the first hunting day. As I said earlier, Sal had all the luck. When we connected with Armand at the end of the hunt, he hadn't gotten his grizzly or even seen one. Later that summer Sal phoned and said, "Hey Cody, the taxidermist can't fix the goat." Ralph Stewart was nice enough to give Sal his full-mount goat hide, as he had shot one earlier with his resident draw.

I stayed in touch with Sal for many more years, until one day he didn't answer the phone anymore. I wondered if it was Mafia related. He was supposed to come the next year for cougar, but he phoned at the last minute and cancelled. My assistant guide, Gordon Rice, who had his own dogs, needed a hunter to replace Sal. When he and I couldn't find one, I took the hunt for myself and paid Gordon. He had a big cat picked out near the Palliser road at the thirty-three-kilometre post.

I met him there on my birthday, and he turned his dogs loose. Within thirty minutes we had the cougar treed. After treeing him, then chasing him out of the tree to be treed again by the dogs, I shot him on the third tree. He had been eating an elk a week, I figured, as I had seen his kills when I was trapping the area. He would have made the Boone and Crockett, but I didn't register him. I had him full mounted by Aasland Taxidermy in Cranbrook.

Sal sent me a picture of his trophy room. It had the big bull elk, the goat and the grizzly, and it should have had the cougar. If I hadn't sold out, I'm sure I could have booked many more "Mafia" hunters.

THE KILLER GRIZZLY OF ALBERT RIVER

In the fall of 1994 while hunting for goat on Goat Mountain with one of my clients, I met Shane Fumerton and his wife, Carey, who were also hunting there. I invited them to base camp for a visit. They were very nice people, so I decided to tell them where to get a Boone and Crockett goat the following fall, if they got a resident draw. Sure enough they were lucky with the draw, but unfortunately, their hunt took a tragic turn.

On October 9, 1995, Shane and his friend Bill Caspell started out to hunt Mount Soderholm, where I had told them I had seen many Boone and Crockett goats. On the climb, though, they got sidetracked by hunting a big bull elk.

They had pedalled their bikes past the road closure on the Albert River to a slide at the fifteen-mile mark, where I had told them to look. Shane's wife, Carey, had stayed back at camp to hunt elk. When they didn't show up by dark, she started to worry. She spent the next three days looking, hoping and even getting other hunters to help. One of them drove past the road closure and found the bikes, but there was no sign of the men.

Finally, four days later, an official search was launched, and a Search and Rescue chopper out of Banff spotted the kill site of the elk.

The following day, they finally contacted me through the RCMP. Carey thanked me when I met her at the bottom of the mountain. When I heard where the kill site was, I noticed right away that it was across the head of the basin from where the goats usually were. This didn't make sense to me, as they were meant to be going after goats. The chopper pilot had spotted a black plastic bag flying around the spot the night before, so they headed back with Search and Rescue and dogs, while Burns and I mounted a ground search from the bottom. We also had two young guides to help us.

It had snowed during the night, and as we climbed the mountain, the snow steadily got deeper. About halfway to the site, I came across a very fresh and very large set of grizzly tracks. I kept climbing, thinking of the blond grizzly that had been giving us so much trouble in the territory. Not long after, I heard shots fired from the helicopter. I saw the conservation officer shoot one cub from where I was.

About an hour later, I saw the chopper make a couple of trips to the bottom, where Carey and the others were waiting. I decided they must have found the guys, so we headed back down. By the time I got there, the search crew had the bodies in an ambulance and the antlers of the elk in the conservation officer's truck. Carey was devastated, and my heart went out to her. From the chopper, the CO had shot two yearling cubs and a small sow. Had the big boar just taken a walk before this all took place? This was on my mind.

The following summer, at Carey's prodding, several of us returned to the kill site to do an investigation. Joining me were the Search and Rescue team from the national park service; James Gary Shelton, who was writing *Bear Attacks: The Deadly Truth*; a family member of Shane's; and the coroner from Golden.

As we put it together, I couldn't help but imagine how fast it would have happened and how helpless they would have felt. There is nothing faster than a charging grizzly that wants possession of a carcass. I had once measured the tracks during a hunt, where the hunter shot one grizzly as another one ran away down a snow slide; it was twenty-seven feet between foot marks. Without a chance of taking a shot, these guys didn't have a hope in hell of surviving. They were in the wrong place with a kill at the wrong time, and there is nothing you can do about that. So many questions remain that will never be answered.

The conclusion of that investigation confirmed my thoughts that a big grizzly boar was more likely responsible for killing the two men and that the sow and cubs had arrived at the kill site later. Well, it wouldn't have made any difference; the search had been delayed for over a day while the searchers waited for government permission to kill the sow and cubs. The full details appeared in James Gary Shelton's book and also in a report put out by the North American Hunting Club. That also left me with the knowledge that I quite likely had a man-killing grizzly in my hunting territory.

I was pretty sure I knew which bear had done the killing. Right from Dad's heyday in the Palliser until I started in 1979, we always had bear problems. This only got worse as the years went by, and more gut piles were evident with the increase in elk numbers. The resident hunters who hunted the Albert River, along with me and other guides in the Palliser and Queen Mary areas, harvested elk and goat by the dozens.

We saw the increase in bear numbers rise rapidly, and large boars showed up to stay. One of these boars was very aggressive. He was a large blond grizzly that in the fall could weigh as much as six hundred to seven hundred pounds. I once met him on the high elk trail on a corner at the head of Fynn Creek, with about fifty feet between us. I had a very close and good look at his face. He was scarred up pretty good from past battles with other bears. He stood his ground on the trail, and I had to spur my big sixteen-hand mule, Jake, ahead to meet him. There were two hunters and a guide behind me, all mounted on horses that weren't afraid of bears. I could tell this big bear didn't want to give up the trail, as he was used to having his way. He never did run, but he ambled into the buckbrush lower down the slide. He had arrived a couple of years earlier. He could have originally come from Banff National Park, Kananaskis or another surrounding area.

One of the guides had had a run-in with him at the bottom of Fynn Creek a year or two earlier. They had shot an elk, and after dressing it out, they went back for a couple of mules. When they got back a few hours later, the big blond grizzly was on the kill. They fired shots in the air and tried to approach with the horses and mules, but the bear stood his ground. They gave up. Later that fall I went back and found the antlers, still in good shape, so I sent them to the hunter.

We were often trailed by grizzlies, as they got to know that where we went, there would be gut piles. You would ride up the trail in the morning, and when you returned that night, there would be bear tracks over yours.

By about 1990 I felt I could recognize most of the bears in the territory. There was a blond sow, normally with two cubs, at the Joffre Creek end; we called her Sundog Sally. There was a black silvertip sow, which also averaged two cubs, around the Tipperary Lake area, and she often frequented the Tipperary Cabin. One night she cleaned us out of the meat and bacon we had stored in a ground cooler. Another night she showed up to a bonanza. We had two bull elk capes, two mule deer capes and a goat hide all ready and salted for transport; they were hanging on the cross beam on the old Tipperary Cabin. Frank and Lorne Thompson had taken the meat and antlers to the meat cutter's in town that same day. With the hunters sleeping in this cabin, and Don Koopmans and Linda in the new cook cabin, no one heard a sound. When we got up in the morning, there was nothing hanging there. The hunters could not believe they hadn't heard anything, as they were so close to the capes hanging a few feet away outside. We scoured the area and found the four capes, all of them with the ears and lips eaten off, but we never did find the goat hide.

The third sow was in the Queen Mary and Albert River area. She was also a silvertip with two cubs on average. I know she was not the same sow as in the Tipperary area, as I saw them in the same year a couple of times, and their cubs were one- and two-year-olds.

Randy Atwood was cooking for me one fall, and he was also breaking a three-year-old mare. When the guides, Dennis Tegart and Frank Thompson, plus Randy and the hunters, arrived at Queen Mary, a big storm rolled in. They kept the horses tied up for the first night because of this, plus the horses were very fat and might try to pull out right away. After Randy got the guys off hunting the next morning, he went to hobble and turn the horses loose. He couldn't find the young mare. He went and checked the trail back to base camp, but there were no tracks. He then scoured the area, but there was no sign.

A day or two had gone by when he went to get water from the lake. Close to shore, he saw a red rock that he had never seen before. It turned out to be the mare. That evening they saddled a horse, and with Dennis pulling it on horseback with a lash rope and the rest pushing it away from shore, they managed to tow it to the other end of the lake. Once there, they worked like hell to get it up on shore. As the days went by, a big grizzly came in and took possession. He stayed that hunt and all through the next hunt before he left just a bone pile. That was everyone's entertainment. He was also a big blond boar.

We will never know for sure which bear killed those men, but the big blond boar was the one seen the most on gut piles or following someone on a pack trail. Doug Goodwin was guiding a hunter and spent the day at the head of the Palliser, watching two young bears feeding on huckleberries. Darryl McLean was at Grizzly Ridge about five miles lower down the Palliser, waiting a bull out. The bull unexpectedly came out in the middle of the day, and the hunter started blazing away. Doug said he heard the shots, and he watched the young bears stand up, listen for a few minutes, then head down the valley. They didn't get lunch that day, as the hunter missed.

A grizzly was harassing a bull one time in the head end of Fynn Creek when Cam MacDonald and I had two hunters up there. It was the heat of the day, and this bull was bugling like hell. As I was bugling him, he started coming very willingly. I spotted the blond grizzly following him about a hundred yards behind. We went ahead and shot the elk anyway. He was so pumped up that it took five shots to bring him down. While we were butchering and caping him out, another bull came up the mountain, bugling like hell. We waited where we were and bugled him within a hundred yards, and the other hunter shot him. He was also an average six point. We finished getting the elk ready for the following day, as we didn't have enough horses to pack them out, and the hunters weren't tough enough to walk all the way back to Tipperary.

The following morning Cam, Terry Brown, Mom and I headed back to get the elk. Mom had never been in that area and wanted to see the country. The hunters stayed in camp to do a little fishing. When we got to the shot-up elk, a grizzly left on the high run. This was lucky, as we didn't have a gun with us. The bear had eaten his fill and buried the rest. The cape and antlers were in good shape. The other elk was in good shape, and the hunters split the meat when we got it back to camp. This hunt happened about fifteen years before the attack, and I wondered if maybe that was the bear, and he had ranged elsewhere for a few years. In all, I guided twelve grizzly hunts, some of them with Darryl McLean, and he guided one by himself. From these we took ten bears, including a wounded one that we never did find, even using dogs, and one that was a miss at a hundred yards.

The spring after the attack, I was issued two grizzly quotas. I phoned Ernie Knight from Virginia, as he had a vendetta with the big blond boar. He booked me right away and brought his friend, whose name I think was Robert. Ervin Morneau came to guide.

The first morning Ervin and Robert went up Lodgepole, and Ernie and I headed for the Albert River. It was about ten in the morning, as I had found that you very seldom saw grizzly or black bears early. We had just crossed the first bridge on the Albert River when, lo and behold, there was a blond grizzly busy digging roots right beside the river in an open cutblock. This was probably why he hadn't heard the truck. We stopped and piled out with my spotting scope and Ernie's rifle. We leaned over the hood of the truck for a perfect rest. The wind was in our favour. Bear distances are hard to judge unless you are very close. We didn't know what sex it was, so we watched for quite a while. I finally decided it was probably a boar and possibly the killer of the Albert River. Ernie was very relaxed by now, and the three-hundred-yard shot was no problem. The bear dropped where he was digging, and I didn't even bother taking my gun when we went to him. He was a seven-and-a-half-square-foot bear, very blond with a great spring coat. After taking pictures, we skinned him out. As I was doing this, I was trying to remember the face of the bear I had met in Fynn Creek on my mule. Anyway, we were happy and headed for Fisher Creek Camp. Ervin and Robert hadn't found anything except large tracks up the main Palliser Road.

A few days later Ervin found the same large tracks up by Sundog Creek, which still had snow, and the two of them went tracking it into Sundog. That same afternoon Ernie and I were on a road down by Cedarville, watching a cutblock for black bear, when two guys came along. I had met them a few times in the fall, road hunting the Palliser, and they were nice guys.

Ernie Knight from Virginia with his blond grizzly. It looked like the Albert River Killer but wasn't.

One of them had a limited grizz draw for the area. We chatted for a while and told them we already had our grizz and Ervin and his hunter were up Sundog chasing tracks. They were nice enough to ask if they could drive on up the Palliser without bothering Ervin, and I said yes. I invited them over to base camp later if they wanted.

They were back in three hours with a bear. They said they had gotten to Fantail Slide and saw a bear across the river on the slide. They hustled across the river and up to the slide. The bear was still there. They shot and missed, and the grizzly just looked at them. The next shot put him down for good. They quickly skinned him out, leaving the feet and head with the hide.

The next morning, when they pulled him out on the tailgate, I said, "That's the bear that killed the guys in the Albert River." He was the right colour and size. And I recognized his face.

THE GRIZZLY THAT ALMOST GOT ME

One season I hadn't found a hunter, so I booked a man from Missouri who I didn't want to take. I needed his money to pay for insurance, my outfitter's licence, taxes on cabin sites and range fees for the horses, just to start the year. He wanted to bring his wife along. She was to hunt black bear and needed a guide, so Darryl McLean came along for the job.

Now this hunter was a pushy peckerwood, so when I got him to base camp about forty miles from the highway, things changed. I made sure that he knew I was the boss or he would have a long walk back to town with his gear and wife in tow. The guy knew how to get on my nerves, and I had to keep him under my thumb constantly.

Darryl was up the Albert River with the hunter's wife when they spotted a grizzly feeding on the leftovers of a wolf kill on an island in the middle of the river. They watched him for a long time, as the noise of the river kept him from noticing.

The next day Darryl took the hunter back to the spot on the river, and I took his wife for black bear. We went to the end of the Palliser Road without seeing anything, but as we headed back, we saw a very large black bear across the river on Fantail Slide. We watched him for a long time, and it seemed that he was going to stay for a while. We decided to go after him, and this meant crossing the Palliser, even though the water was high with spring melt. I had some running shoes in the truck, so I put them on, grabbed my Trapper Nelson backpack, and away we went. I didn't bother with my rifle, as it was only a black bear. When we got to the river, the wife crawled on my back, and I held my pack and her gun in front of me. The water was to my waist, and I needed her weight to hold me down in the rapid current. She got her feet wet too, but we safely made it across.

Next was the steep climb up to the slide. I had climbed here many times in the past and knew the best elk trails. When we reached the bottom, we spotted the bear feeding in the buckbrush near the top of the slide, about three hundred yards away. There was a veteran fir about four feet across on the butt. she got comfortable and used the base for a rest. I was watching, and when I could see the bear's shoulder through the brush, I told her to shoot. *Boom!* The bear started racing down the slide out of the brush. When he was in full view, I could see he was a smaller bear and he had clearly been hit. He saw us and swung to our left toward the timber.

Suddenly, out of the same brush above us came the big black; he was headed right toward us on a high run. I grabbed her gun, put another bullet in the barrel, aimed and started hollering. She jumped behind me as I screamed at the bear, "One more step and I will kill you!" I was just about to pull the trigger when he veered to the left where the other bear had gone.

This was damn exciting, and I think the wife almost peed herself. I know my butthole was sucked up tighter than a bull's arse in fly time. We settled down and went and found the bear she had hit. We didn't have a camera, so I just skinned him out but left the feet and head in. I put him on the pack board, and we headed for the river. I had a damn good load on my back with the extra weight, but I managed. That evening Darryl and the hunter returned, having sat at the wolf kill site all day, but nothing had shown.

A few more days went by and Linda had a good feeling about Lodgepole Creek. We jumped in the truck and the hunter, his wife, Linda and I went for a drive. There were five slides in Lodgepole, across the valley from the logging road. They were easy to see, as the roadside had been logged out. Sure enough, about four hundred yards from the bottom of the centre slide was a grizzly digging in the snow. This was the only snow left from an earlier avalanche, and I figured there was probably a dead goat in it. It was late in the afternoon, so we had to hustle.

We left the girls watching, and down through the windfalls and logging debris we went. The hunter was bitching as usual, and I had to tell him to shut up if he wanted the bear. We reached the bottom and started the climb up a chute, just right of the bear. Once we were in the chute the grizz couldn't see us, and as we climbed I would look over the edge to check on him.

When we reached about sixty yards, I stopped. I prepped the hunter and put a bullet in my 30-06 also. I had the bear that tried to bite my knee in mind, so I wasn't taking any chances. The bear was intent on digging and was unaware of us, plus the wind was in our favour. When he was ready, I whistled. This brought the bear's head up. He was broadside and a perfect shot. *Boom!* went his gun. The grizzly flew over backwards and started sliding down the snow toward us. I had my rifle trained on him, but he appeared lifeless. The hunter put another round in the barrel. The bear slid off the snow and into the draw about twenty yards above us. I could see blood on his brisket and hair missing. We watched for a couple minutes and then congratulated each other. That was the only time that hunter was half nice.

Suddenly, the bear jumped up, looked at us and climbed out of the chute so fast I didn't have time to shoot. He headed for the timber as I scrambled up to where I could get a shot. It was too late, as he had entered the alders at the edge of the slide. I forgot about the hunter and trailed the bear into the big spruce. When I got in a ways, it was too dark, so I retreated. We crawled back up to the truck. The girls had seen it all and couldn't believe the bear got up and ran away. Back to camp we went. I was sure that when I went back in the morning, I would find the bear dead.

The next morning, I had the hunter up and ready to go by daylight. We drove back to Lodgepole and I left him in the truck to watch the slide, down from where the bear had gone into the timber. He didn't want to hike through the snow and was already bitching about how much work it would be for him to come with me. Darryl was gone somewhere, so I was on my own. I retraced my steps from the night before, and when I got to where the bear had been lying in the chute, I found little pieces of bone on the ground. With this, I was sure I would find a lifeless carcass in the timber.

As I entered the big spruce, the snow was about four feet deep. It was spring snow, so I only sank about six inches.

The tracks were easy to follow. I walked along slowly, gun pointed ahead, bullet in the barrel and safety off. I kept expecting a dead bear, but about two hundred yards in I found a bed full of blood. The tracks continued as I followed for about another two hundred yards. There was another bed with less blood. Now I was really starting to feel uneasy. I psyched myself up as if I was getting on a real rank bull and continued tracking. The next bed was on the top side of a big spruce and very fresh.

I looked ahead for a long time, trying to see the tracks through the trees. I was about to start again when I heard a shot from where I had left the hunter. I thought he must have shot at or killed the grizzly. It must have moved out onto the slide and low enough to be in range for him. With this thought in mind, I headed for the slide. A big spruce about 150 feet long had fallen across a ravine I had to cross. It was covered with the hard-packed snow and was easier to cross than crawling down and back up the ravine. I crossed this safely and walked out on to the slide. I looked across the valley to where I had left the truck and the hunter. Nothing. I looked down the snow-covered slide area and saw no tracks.

What the hell is going on? I asked myself. I started down the slide, watching for tracks in the snow spots. I reached the bottom, seeing no sign of tracks except old moose tracks. I climbed up to the road and couldn't hear my truck. I hollered but got no response. Other than the sound off the creek I had just jumped across, there was little sound. A willow grouse beat his mating sound in the distance, and a blue jay squawked at me, but that was it. I started walking toward camp. After about two miles I heard a truck coming, so I sat down to wait, resting my tired legs.

Linda came around the corner with the hunter and his wife. I confronted him when they stopped, but Linda said, "I already gave him supreme hell. He's a stupid ignorant asshole."

I asked, "What was the shot all about?"

He said, "That was to let you know I went back to camp for lunch."

I threatened to drag him out of the truck and beat the shit out of him. The deal on this hunt was he gave me four thousand dollars for the hunt and another two thousand when he got his bear. I needed that extra money, so I had to prove to him that he got his bear. I jumped in the back of the truck and we headed for camp. By the time we got there, I had a plan.

I jumped out of the truck box and told Linda to go to town and get Jimmy Hagan, a dog man with excellent bear dogs. If she couldn't get him, I told her to get Dave Langridge, who was also an excellent dog hunter. Jimmy had guided for Dad, and David had gone to school with me. I just decided I was going to get pissed. Later the hunter's wife came in and made them supper, but I didn't talk to him.

The next morning, very early, Linda was back in camp. She wasn't alone. There was Jimmy and his dogs, Ervin Morneau, Darryl, and Ralph Stewart and his whole crew. Everyone was armed to the teeth and loaded for bear. We headed back to the area where I last saw the tracks. We climbed up the slide I had just come down the day before. Linda, the asshole and his wife stayed with the trucks to watch.

When we got to the spot where I had crossed the big spruce above the ravine the day before, the dogs went nuts.

Jimmy said, "Get ready, boys; he's right here close." He turned the dogs loose and they charged toward the ravine.

Minutes later out came the grizzly, with the dogs biting at his hind legs.

Suddenly, a thought flashed through my mind: *Shit!* The bear had been right there when the hunter had fired the shot. He was plenty alive. Hell! Maybe that son of a bitch had saved my life.

The bear charged out in front of us, oblivious to our presence, and sat down on his ass to fight off the dogs. Ervin was in the lead and closest to him. He was trying to get closer so he could get a shot without hitting a dog.

Suddenly, the bear saw Ervin. He jumped to his feet and raced past us, headed for the bottom. I was ahead of Ervin now, and we raced down the mountain following the dogs. They went straight as an arrow to the creek. When we got to the creek, the dogs were running up and down the creek, jumping back and forth from side to side. There was no snow now.

Finally, Jim and the boys showed up. Jim caught his dogs and we worked the creek both ways to no avail. We finally gave up, as we were all wet and tired. When everyone left the camp, I asked them to get hold of David Langridge, as Jimmy had to work the next day.

Sure enough, early the next morning Dave showed up with his hounds. We drove back to the bottom of Lodgepole, and his dogs started baying in the back of his truck. He turned them loose and they headed into the logging area, baying like hell. Around and around they went for hours. After most of the day went by with nothing indicating a cornered bear, David caught up to the dogs and we loaded them up. He headed for home.

That evening Brian McKersie from Radium showed up in camp. He had heard the story, and he wanted to try his dog out but keep him on a leash. It was some kind of terrier. We spent the morning combing where we thought the bear had gone, but it was to no avail. With this last try, I told this hunter that the hunt was over and he owed me the extra two thousand for a wounded bear.

I let Linda take them to the airport, as I wanted him to know I didn't like his attitude. I never let on to him that he probably saved my life with his shot to tell me he was going back to camp for lunch. The grizzly must have been so close when he fired that shot, and this bear was still plenty alive, the way he ran away from us. The chances he was waiting for me were extremely good, and my chances of killing him at close range were extremely slim.

Thanks, asshole; I'm still alive. But I'll never tell you.

ZIMBABWE, AFRICA: THE GUIDE BECOMES THE HUNTER

I belonged to the Guide Outfitters Association of British Columbia, the Sierra Club, the Rocky Mountain Elk Foundation, the Mule Deer Foundation and the Safari Club International. The BC chapter of the Safari Club was started by Hank Campsall, Albert Cooper and Odd Assland of Assland Taxidermy, and probably others I didn't know. All were well-known outfitters in the East Kootenay. Years earlier Hank and Albert had taken me to my first SCI show to book my first hunters from the Minnesota area.

We were all chewing the fat at one of our regular meetings at Odd's house in Cranbrook, where I was the youngest. The guys were always devising ways to get money from the American chapters for different things like elk habitat, et cetera. With this American money, they booked booths in different states. Hank and Albert had a lot of SCI hunters from Minneapolis, and Odd had some from Washington. There was an SCI show coming up in Spokane, but everyone was busy, so they asked if I would go. Hell yes I would, as I wanted more exposure for myself.

Money was tighter than a bull's arse in fly time, so I borrowed the next fall's hunting deposits and away Linda and I went.

It was the spring of 1989 when we arrived at a big complex in Spokane. As we set up the booth in the coliseum, we realized that we had left the slide projector behind. These were the days before outfitters used videos to sell hunts. I went to the management to see if they had one on hand. They did, but a guy by the name of Frank McCourt from Zimbabwe, Africa, had already borrowed it.

As the day went by, I showed my album pictures, and three guys came along who were very interested. It was time to track down the projector and this Frank fellow from Zimbabwe. He had a hunting concession in the Mantiki Hills and also quotas for Cape buffalo around Lake Kariba. I introduced myself and asked if I could show my slides to the three hunters. We watched his slides for a while, then put mine in. The three hunters got excited and decided to book with me. Frank, seeing my pictures, commented that I had some very big bulls and he would like to hunt them someday.

I said, "I just want to hunt anything, preferably kudu, in Zimbabwe. Want to trade a hunt?"

"Yes, I do," he said, with a big smile and a handshake.

Well, that's how my brother Dennis, Ervin Morneau, Linda and I wound up in Africa. Frank had asked me to make a group of three or four for the hunting party. Ervin was ready right off the bat, and Dennis agreed as soon as I phoned him. I made the arrangements, and the following June we flew out of Edmonton to Heathrow, England. Frank had asked me to send our deposits to a friend of his in Detroit, because he wanted to keep his money in the US. The government in Zimbabwe was taking foreign currency and charging an 800 percent tax or something ridiculous like that.

The trip was in daylight, and the flight took us over Greenland. After a very short sleep somewhere in England, off we went for another twelve hours direct to Harare, Zimbabwe, which is the capital city. On the flight the view was unbelievable, especially crossing the Sahara. You would see miles of sand, then suddenly an oasis or the occasional camel train. The landscape went from grey to green very rapidly. This was the edge of the Congo. It would be cloudy for a while, then back to desert as we approached Zimbabwe.

We landed, and Frank and his wife were waiting. We spent our first night with them in Harare. Their beautiful home and yard were surrounded by a high fence with barbed wire on top. Everyone went to bed with jet lag, but I was up very early, hyper with excitement. Our day was night and vice versa now. I went out in the yard, not wanting to disturb anyone. There were two men on their knees picking grass. I said hi and didn't get an answer. I looked around for a while, then Frank called me to come in for breakfast.

I asked, "Why are those guys picking grass?"

His reply was, "They're my lawn mowers and caretakers."

Welcome to Africa, I thought.

After a great breakfast, we loaded up in two Willys Jeeps. Frank's wife drove one with Linda and Dennis, and Frank drove Ervin and me. About six hours later we stopped for lunch at a bunch of grass huts by the highway. We entered a hut with wooden tables and a dirt floor. As we headed for some tables, Frank stopped to talk to another professional hunter who went by the name Talkie, which is what they call guides and outfitters. As he was talking and we were waiting, a big fellow sitting at Talkie's table kept looking at me. I had seen his face before but couldn't remember where. Finally, he said to me, "I've seen you somewhere before. Where are you from?" I told him I was an outfitter from BC, and he replied, "I remember you now. You were at a sports show in Minneapolis, and I talked to you about a hunt."

"It's a small world," I replied.

We arrived in the camp in the Mantiki Hills late that day. It was a beautiful camp, with open, grass-covered rooms for the hunters. They had about a six-foot wall and then were open to the roof. There were no mosquitoes and only few flies, which the little lizards kept down. They were very colourful and were everywhere. Linda and I had our own beds, as did Dennis and Ervin.

About a hundred yards from our area were the locals' huts. These were grass covered, round in shape and slept quite a few people. They slept on the dirt floor, covered by grass and reeds, and they cooked outside on a fire. They ate mainly corn meal, and they trapped small animals, as they were not allowed guns.

The first morning of hunting, Frank sent Dennis and Ervin to a different area with his assistant guide and their African trackers. Linda stayed in camp with Frank's wife, and Frank, my tracker and I headed out to check on the different African camps in his concession. The tracker would stand in the back of the open Jeep, roll tobacco in newspaper, hang on to the cross bar and use the wind to keep it smoking as we drove along.

After an hour or so, we came across a herd of about fifty impalas. Frank stopped and said, "Shoot one. I need to drop off some fresh meat for the next camp." I had to wait awhile until I could shoot one without killing another one behind it. I was using Frank's .270, as that was easier than bringing one along with me. I finally had a clear shot as a doe stepped forward, so I pulled the trigger. The herd ran away, and after a few hundred yards the doe dropped dead. We drove up to it, and as the tracker and I jumped out of the Jeep, I pulled out my small knife to start gutting the thing.

"Whoa," said Frank. "That's the tracker's job."

As I stood there, I was surprised to see the tracker drag the antelope into the back of the Jeep. It probably weighed about 150 pounds, but Frank told me not to help him. Then away we went, with the tracker smoking his newspaper stogie and a gut-shot impala in the back of the Jeep. Now I definitely knew I was in a different world and not up the Palliser. As we drove along, it got hotter and hotter. The impala started to bloat and stink increasingly more.

We finally arrived at a village, and Frank talked to some locals in their language. They dragged the bloated carcass out of the Jeep and disappeared into a shed that Frank had there. I couldn't help but think we would never treat our dead game this way. The rest of the day consisted of checking out villages, with Frank talking to the locals in their language. We saw lots of wildlife, but no kudus, which was what I was interested in. We saw lots of giraffes, loads of impala and other small antelope.

The following day Frank, the tracker and I headed out in the dark. We arrived at our destination and started walking to a water hole, which was quite a ways from the Jeep. Frank put the tracker in the lead. As we headed out through the grass and brush, he kept beating the ground ahead of him with shooting sticks.

When we finally stopped, I whispered to Frank, "What's he beating the grass for?"

His reply was, "To keep us from getting bit by snakes. We have some very poisonous ones here and big pythons."

We arrived at the water hole and watched it until noon. We saw warthogs, zebras and a few nyala, an antelope on quota. We went back to camp for lunch, which we would do on most days to come. The following day was much the same, and as it was so interesting, the days flew by.

The third day we went hiking after a couple of kudu we had spotted. I had my spotting scope, and even at quite a distance I could tell they weren't very big. We decided to have a closer look, and as the ground was very rocky, the tracker had a tough time in his worn-out sandals. I turned the bulls down when we got within shooting range. If compared to elk, they would be like a small four or five point.

Frank went and checked on Dennis and Ervin. Dennis had an impala and Ervin had shot a gorgeous big kudu, an impala and a warthog.

Frank decided to take Dennis for his Cape buffalo at a camp at Lake Kariba. He said this was a real tourist camp and that they also raised crocodiles there. Linda and Ervin went along, and I stayed back to try to get a kudu.

I went with the assistant guide, Kiki, and my tracker to another water hole that day. Each of us had a tracker with us as part of the hunt. They did all the work. We spent the morning watching a water hole, but no kudu. We did see warthogs, zebra, lots of impala and eland, which were huge antelope weighing in at about one thousand pounds or more. You could hear them coming from half a mile, as their ankles clicked loudly as they walked. I could have shot one very easily but couldn't afford the trophy fee plus shipping and mounting, so I had to pass.

Kiki and the tracker went to another water hole to look for a kudu and left me by myself at the first water hole. There were piles of monstrous round boulders scattered across the terrain. I don't know how they got there, as they must have been millions of years old and from a different time. I was hiding in the shade of these, watching the water, when in the distance I heard a slight hum. It was so quiet in that country, as there were no jets or highways, and only the odd small plane might pass in the distance. I couldn't figure out what the hell it was and was starting to get nervous. The hum continued to increase in volume and got closer. I didn't know what the hell to do, except stand my ground. Suddenly the sky turned black as millions of bees flew over me, some as close as ten feet. I froze and damn near crapped my drawers. I had never expected anything like this and was almost weak. Hell, I'd take on a grizzly and know what to expect, but this was different.

Finally, the guys returned, and when I explained what had happened, they laughed. "It's just bees migrating," was Kiki's answer. "They won't hurt you."

A couple of days later, Dennis returned with his big Cape buffalo. Ervin and Linda were with him and had lots of stories to tell. Dennis had shot his bull at four hundred yards with his .475 H&H Magnum, out of a herd of about five hundred.

While in Zimbabwe, Cody's brother Dennis, under the guidance of local hunter Frank McCourt, shot a Cape buffalo. It was later mounted and still hangs in the Clinton Hotel to this day.

The next day Dennis, Ervin and I went out in my camp, the Mantiki Hills Camp. I finally saw a big kudu through the trees. It was only about a hundred yards away. I only had an offhand shot and took a chance through the brush. I felt good, but I must have hit a branch, as the kudu ran away. Ervin and I were gone like bullets after him. We picked up his tracks from where he had bolted and started after him at a trot. The local trackers couldn't keep up because their sandals were worn out. Kiki let Ervin and I do our thing, and we tracked it to the top of a rise. There was no blood, but we were hot on his trail. Sure enough, he had quit running and was below us about five hundred yards. Kiki informed me that he was out of the concession, so I couldn't shoot him. That was my last chance for a kudu.

The next day Dennis decided to take an eland. We all went to the water hole that they had been drinking at. They came in like usual, ankles clicking as they walked. After they drank, Dennis took aim with Frank's .270 and shot. The biggest bull ran about a hundred yards and tipped over. When we got up close, we realized just how massive the animal was.

While we were taking pictures, Kiki went back to camp for another Jeep. When he got back, he had more locals with him. They dug a trench for the back tires up to the eland. They then pushed, pulled and winched the animal into the back of the Jeep. The animal was as big as the Jeep. With all this weight, the Jeep was high centred. They then pulled this Jeep out with the other one. Loaded to the gunnels, literally, we headed for camp. In camp, Frank had a steel cross pole about twenty feet high with an electric winch. He started the generator and started winching up the animal by the hind legs.

The locals started skinning it from the hind legs down, and when they reached the entrails, we couldn't believe what we saw. These poor guys were so meat hungry, they ate the tripe (the fat surrounding the guts) as they worked. We knew then we were far removed from our past. We had a good feed of fresh eland that night. Frank sold the meat at Harare, so the locals only got the leftovers.

One of the things about camp was it was so peaceful. You could go to sleep at night with no worries. You might hear the odd leopard roaring in the distance. You could eat all you wanted. You had clean clothes every morning, and you knew you were going to have a safe day.

One afternoon, one of my trackers' wives came into camp from her village, which was over ten miles away. She had walked for hours across open country to tell her husband that she'd had twins and one had died at birth. Frank let her stay the night, but in the morning he took her to where we were hunting that day, which was in the direction of her village, and dropped her off at the end of the road. The last I saw of her, she was walking off in the distance with not even a stick for defence. I'm sure she picked one up along the way because of snakes.

On the second to last day, Kiki and I went to a small dammed lake, where we had seen a record-book impala. As we waited, a warthog with piglets came racing out of the brush into the clearing by the dam. There was a leopard chasing them, and he was about to catch the last piglet when the mother rapidly swapped ends, and the leopard skidded to a halt, then sat on its rump and watched them run away.

An hour or two later, the impalas showed up. They were across the dam and about three hundred yards away. I laid down with Frank's .270 and picked out the buck. One shot and it was all over. He was a Roland and Ward trophy buck, comparable to our Boone and Crockett.

With this the hunt was over. Linda gave a blanket to the wife of one of the trackers. When Dennis, Ervin and I went to tip a hundred dollars to each tracker, Frank took the money. He said they would get drunk and go crazy, so it was best that he gave them a little bit at a time.

Everyone, including Linda, had left a day earlier than me in one Jeep back to Frank's house in Harare. Kiki was to take me to a small airport a day later and I would catch up. As Frank couldn't get bullets in Zimbabwe, he had asked us to bring a legal amount for him. We brought him as many as was legal for his .270. When we were driving to the small airport, I suddenly remembered I

Cody's impala was a Rowland Ward trophy buck, the African equivalent of the North American Boone and Crockett rankings.

still had some bullets in my duffle. When I told Kiki, he screeched to a halt, took the shells and hid them in the bush, marking the location so he could find them later. He said that only Frank could transport them off the hunting concession.

When I got to the airport, I tipped Kiki and asked the pilot what it cost to fly to Harare. He said thirty American dollars or something like that. I said, "I'll give you fifty for a little extra flying." Away we went, and I got to see what the country really looked like. We saw tons of animals, as we were very close to the ground. What a way to end a hunt.

With the trip over, Frank arranged for our trophies to be shipped to Edmonton. Ervin's warthog got confiscated for some reason, but everything else arrived safely. My sister, June Burrows, was into taxidermy at the time, and she later mounted everything. Dennis's Cape buffalo, eland and impala hang in the Clinton Hotel to this day.

We said our goodbyes and flew to London. We were going to stay a few days and look around, but it was so expensive, it was cheaper to change our flights than to stay more than two nights. The flight home was in the dark, so the excitement was over. What a culture shock.

THE TRAIL TAKES A TWIST

BY ANDY

In early April 2018 Cody decided to take a holiday from the snow that still surrounded his home in Winfield, Alberta. Cody had moved there the previous year from the valley he loved, to be closer to his daughters and siblings and also because valley real estate prices had become unaffordable. With its scenic splendor, the Columbia Valley had become a vacation playground for wealthy Albertans, thereby driving up land prices to the point that a lot of locals could no longer afford to live there. While he missed the valley, Cody enjoyed spending a lot of quality time with his daughters and grandkids, plus he was closer to his younger brother, Garrett, and many old friends.

Cody stopped in the valley for a few days and then made his way to the Okanagan, first visiting his sister Sherri in Kelowna, then coming to our place in Summerland to spend a few days working on the book and just kicking back. We reminisced about old times, talked about new times and drank a lot of beer. We also discussed where we wanted the book to go and the next few chapters. We didn't do a lot of work, because we were having a good time just hanging out. Cody loved the fact that spring was in full force in Summerland and the temperature was in the high teens. As he rose earlier than the rest of us, he would always head out for a morning walk before we got up. One day he asked me about the small mountains to the north and west of us. I told him the one to the north was Rattlesnake Mountain, and Cartwright Mountain was to the west.

He said, "I'm gonna climb one tomorrow." I suggested Cartwright and told him where the trailhead was.

The next morning I awoke to the sound of the front door closing and knew Cody was out for his morning walk. The rest of us got up, and half an hour later, I had a coffee in hand when my phone rang. It was Cody.

"Richards, come out to your backyard. Bring your binoculars and look up on Cartwright." So I did, and there he was, just below the top, walking back and forth and waving at me.

I thought, *You son of a bitch! Now I'm going to have to climb that.*

When he got back to the house, Cody pulled a handful of coarse blond hair out of his pocket and said, "Grizzly hair. I found it on a barbwire fence near the top." Although we have had multiple black bears in our yard, a grizzly this close to town is quite rare. However, I had no doubt he was correct.

Even though he must have practically run up that hill, he admitted his legs were pretty rubbery on the way down. It ended up that he wasn't done with his exercise.

Before continuing on to the coast, the next day Cody headed south to Okanagan Falls for dinner and a visit with his good friend Alan Neville and his wife, Georgia. By all accounts, they had a huge dinner. Afterward, when Cody thought he'd be

Cody at the fossil beds in the Palliser Territory during a trip with his daughter Ashley. Cody would continue to spend time in the land that he loved long after he sold the territory.

sitting back and relaxing, Alan said, "Let's go for a walk and find some bighorn sheep." Cody agreed, anticipating a short stroll, but instead Alan led him up another small mountain. By the end of the day, and twenty thousand steps later according to his phone, the boy was pooped!

The next day Cody headed to the coast for what he hoped would be a couple of days of fishing. Unfortunately, the weather took a turn for the worse and he didn't get out, but he had a good visit with his friend Darryl McLean, who had guided for him multiple times.

A few days later, they came back to the Okanagan and stopped at Cody's sister Sherri's house. Cody was tired of travelling, so my wife, Deena, and I headed up there for a short visit.

The one thing I noticed was that Cody seemed quite tired. We talked about the book a little more and then left for home. Cody would head home the next day, with an overnight stop to visit his sister-in-law, Lorie, in Little Fort on the way.

I called Cody a few days later to talk a bit more about the book. He was excited about an upcoming summer trip to the fossil beds and a hunt he was planning in the fall. We talked about the next chapter and where we wanted to go with the book. I recall that as we ended our conversation, he told me that he had really enjoyed the whole trip, but he was tuckered right out.

The following week we received a phone call letting us know that Cody had passed away, unexpectedly, from natural causes, surrounded by his daughters and in the hearts of his granddaughters and those he loved. I made a promise that his story would be told.

Every time I went out back to work on the garden over the next week, I would look up on Cartwright Mountain and picture him waving at me from up near the top, and I would shed a tear or two. I ended up climbing the mountain to that very same spot. Cody was always good at pushing me.

Cody's daughters and siblings organized a celebration of life in Invermere. Although he had recently moved to Alberta to be closer to family, Cody's heart was always in the Columbia Valley. The celebration truly did Cody proud. Many of his trophy mounts were on display, along with his saddle and gear, plus an example of a mule pack complete with a double-diamond hitch. A brilliant slide show to his favourite music was shown on a big screen, and this brought both tears and laughter to the over five hundred people who attended. His sister Susan sang one of his favourite hill songs, and many told stories that reflected on the man and who he was. After the meal, a band played, and there was dancing, drinking and a whole lot of laughter, just like Cody would have wanted. For me and many others, the evening brought back memories and reunited folks who hadn't seen each other in up to forty years. Cody would have liked that.

I've had time now to deal with the sadness of losing someone who meant so much to me, and while I still find it hard to write this chapter, I'm so glad to have called Cody my friend. His friendship during my formative years helped me become the man I am today—and, I believe, a better one just from knowing him. I know that he touched many people in the same way.

Cody's story will now continue in my voice, but I will endeavour to tell it in the way he would have.

THE END OF THE DREAM

Since 1979 the Palliser River Guides and Outfitters, under Cody's ownership, had an unprecedented success rate of 85 percent in elk hunts and an amazing 100 percent in goat hunts. Everything had been stacked in Cody's favour, with a burgeoning elk population that started in the late seventies and continued into the early nineties. The Palliser River territory possessed the spectacular vistas that enhanced any hunting adventure, and his reputation provided him with an eager customer base. He had a full contingent of experienced guides staffed by family and rodeo friends, and all his ducks seemed to be in line. Because of his high rate of successful hunts, Cody generally had all the hunter bookings his business could handle, and he received top dollar for his hunts. While the money was significant, so were the expenses, and Cody would always have to work off-season in logging or operating heavy equipment. While working the long hours that bush work requires, Cody would still have to look after booking summer trips and the fall hunting season. Simply put, by the early nineties, even with the high level of energy he possessed, Cody was starting to burn out. The life he loved dearly was taking its toll, both on his family and on his health.

Cody also recognized that another factor that was beyond his control was coming into play. Since the peak during the mid-to late eighties, the elk population started showing a decline in the early nineties. Cody started seeing more wolf sign and more evidence of wolf kills. He also noted an increase in the grizzly population at the same time, which benefitted the spring hunt but would end up a factor in the waning elk population. By 1993 Cody had made the agonizing decision to sell the territory and business. This was a difficult decision for him, as he had spent a huge part of his life riding and hunting this area that he loved with a passion. A fellow named Gord Burns had made Cody an offer to buy and had given a deposit. He intended to work with Cody and learn the business while he searched for investors to complete the purchase. After some delays, the purchase was completed in 1995, with Cody staying on to help run the business for an additional two years.

One achievement that Cody was particularly proud of was partnering in the eighties with a local game biologist, Bob Jamieson, and a doctor from Cranbrook, Dr. Allan Askey, in getting the Palliser and surrounding area designated as an official protected BC Forest Service Wilderness Area. After a few decades of intense logging throughout the whole region, this special and unique area was under threat, and only the supreme efforts from this group saved it from the chainsaws and resulted in the area being designated as the Height of the Rockies Provincial Park in 1995. In the next chapter, Bob Jamieson will give his account on that effort and his educated take on the factors that resulted in the sudden and dramatic decline of the elk population.

VICTORY AND LOSS

BY BOB JAMIESON, RETIRED GAME BIOLOGIST

I first saw the Palliser in 1973 when I came to BC from Alberta. I had taken a job as a biologist in Cranbrook. I had to tidy up some concerns in Banff, where I was living then, and rather than drive back, I got someone to drop me off in the Kananaskis Country. I walked up and over a pass into the Spray River valley in the south end of Banff National Park and then south over Palliser Pass and into BC and into the most beautiful wild valley I had ever seen. The sand bars along the river were covered in elk, moose and grizzly tracks, plus there were goats on the mountains above. I hiked down to Joffre Creek, went up Joffre, down the Middle Fork and out to Whiteswan Lake. In those days most of that country was still wild, and I fell in love with it all.

A couple of years later, I was skiing at Big Mountain in Montana, and after a day on the slopes, I sat down on the sundeck beside a big guy who happened to be a doctor in Cranbrook. His name was Dr. Allan Askey. He would alter my life, and Cody's, in a major way. We got talking, and it turned out that he also loved to hike in the country along the Continental

Divide. Then we got to bitching about the logging that was proceeding there and shrinking the wild country remaining along the divide. Thus began the fight to create the Height of the Rockies and Elk Lakes Provincial Parks, which now protect the heads of the Palliser, Middle Fork and Elk Rivers. It was a long journey. Fifteen years.

We wanted to see the country left as it was, wild and beautiful and just a bit difficult to get to. We wanted to make it a BC Forest Service–administered "wilderness area," where hunting and trapping and all such uses would continue, but that wasn't obvious to everyone. We were having a meeting when in came Doreen and Jim Tegart, the outfitter in the Palliser then, and June Tegart and Pete Burrows, who was the trapper there in those days. They came loaded for bear. They didn't understand that they were part of what we wanted to protect and retain in the Palliser. Now Cody, who wasn't in the picture at that time, wasn't a big guy. If he turned sideways, you couldn't even see him. His dad Jim, on the other hand, was the opposite, a very big guy. Going nose to nose with him was an interesting experience. I can clearly remember how Jim's facial features slowly changed as he realized that we were on the same side and were trying to maintain the country as it was, including outfitters and outfitting families like the Tegarts.

So we drew some maps, talked with government folks and found people who also loved that country, and then we created the Palliser Wilderness Society. It was amazing how many people came out of the woodwork and helped out. We realized that Allan Askey and I had some energy for this, but we didn't have the political smarts required to deal with the people in Victoria. They were a long way away in those days, though sometimes I think they are even farther away now. We somehow got in touch with a wilderness advocate from the coast by the name of Ric Careless. He was keen to help, but we needed some money to make trips to Victoria and pay Ric for his full-time involvement in this.

At this point Cody had taken over the outfit from his dad. Allan, Cody and I were sitting around at some point, trying to figure out our next moves, when Cody announced that he would provide the funding to put Ric to work. We didn't make that known, since there was an obvious financial advantage for Cody, but that was the least of his reasons for doing it. He loved the country just like the rest of us. So, if you go up the Middle Fork or the Palliser and love the fact that you still have to hike or ride to get into that country, you have Cody to thank.

Back in the 1970s some government agency put together some maps of Canada that were meant to express the "tourism potential" of areas across Canada in terms of spectacular mountains, glaciers, alpine lakes, et cetera. The very best areas for such attractions were painted red on the map. The map for Alberta and BC had two big red blobs. One was in the Lake Louise area, and the other was in the Palliser/Middle Fork/Upper Elk. Based on this we made the argument that this area should be protected.

In addition, the Height of the Rockies in those days had quite amazing numbers of wildlife, especially mountain goats, elk, moose and bears. We estimated that there were twelve hundred mountain goats in the area, several hundred moose and elk and deer, and about a hundred bighorn sheep on the Elk River side. The country was amazing in early September in those days. I remember being camped in a high basin in the upper Middle

Fork, and at dusk I bugled from a high point where I could look down into the valley. Nine bulls answered me. Life was perfect then, with nine bulls wanting to fight with me and with each other, the sun going down and turning the Limestone Lakes into little pools of gold, a mountain breeze on my face and a warm sleeping bag just a short walk down the ridge.

There were all kinds of good reasons for leaving the country alone, but of course nothing was rational about the fifteen-year battle to simply leave a bit of high country alone. There was meeting after meeting, I got nasty phone calls, and I was run off the road by logging truck drivers who knew my old half-ton. There were other loggers who, when no one was looking, stuffed money in my shirt pocket to help finance the fight. It all came to a head when the forest company involved went to the city council in Invermere and told them that the creation of the wilderness area would result in the loss of several hundred logging jobs. That was an outright lie. We had worked with the BC Forest Service and had worked out the numbers. They were not large and certainly not several hundred. Someone on council called me about it, and in a fit of smartness, which was not common for me in those days, rather than rant over the phone, I told him to call the BC Forest Service and ask them. Which is what they did. No one likes being lied to, and that is what tipped the balance. In the end several town councillors provided letters of support for the proposal, along with all of the rod and gun clubs in the valley and many others.

At this point we were all just plain worn out, and I had actually given up when, in 1987, they announced that BC's first Wilderness Area was to be established.

It was a hell of a thing. Cody organized a big party up at base camp, with lots of food and music, on a perfect clear mountain night. It was a wonderful time; there must have been a hundred people there, all mountain folks of various kinds, from naturalists (that was before we invented "enviros") to hunters, outfitters and others who just plain loved their mountains wild.

Then it all went Tegart on us. Jim was pretty drunk, and Cody and I decided that we needed to put him to bed. Jim wasn't having any of it. So there we were, Cody and me on either side of Jim, trying to guide him toward the cabin and a nice warm bed. We were standing on the edge of the river, arguing and shouting about who was going to put whom to bed, and Jim took a swing at me. (He had very big fists; I can remember one of them coming at me!) Cody tried to block it, and all three of us tipped over and fell in the river. So there we were, lying in a foot of water, disturbing the poor fish, soaking wet, looking up at the stars, some cowboy music playing in the background. It doesn't get more western, or more Tegart, than that. We crawled out of the river, laughing ourselves sick. We sat there on the bank, and Jim said, "You know, boys, I think I will go to bed."

Following that, Cody became a fixture in the upper Palliser, and I went north and ended up running one of the big Stone sheep areas up there. Ric went on to other adventures, and Al went back to doctoring. But none of us will ever forget those days.

Those were the salad days in the Palliser. Elk numbers were through the roof. It was a perfect time, if you were a hunter looking for a winter's meat, or just someone who loved to sit under a tree on a moonlit night and listen to the big bulls sing. In the morning you could get up to the sound of horse bells, then ride down the trail and look up to see goats on damn near every mountain. But then of course, things had to change.

Elk had been common in our valley in the very old days, around 1800. David Thompson shipped "hundreds" of red deer (the European name for elk) hides back over the mountains. In his daily journal, he wrote that at one point in 1808, he stopped at Skookumchuck Flats (south of Canal Flats, north of Wasa Lake) and killed a "red stag" and saw a wolf. We have no record of their numbers from that era or for much of the 1800s. The gold rush at the Wild Horse likely spelled the end of significant numbers of elk in the East Kootenay, as people there tried to feed themselves. They were a long way from any other sources of red meat.

By 1900 there were only two small groups of elk left, one group in the Flathead, maybe fifty to a hundred head, and another hundred head or so at the head of the Elk and White Rivers. An early explorer and conservationist, William Hornaday, came up to hunt in the Elk Valley in 1902 and saw sign of a few elk. He was from the New York Zoological Society, and he recommended to officials in Victoria that some of this country needed to be protected for the elk. The end result was the White River Game Reserve, which covered most of the Upper Elk and Upper White River drainages. No hunting was allowed there for several decades.

The elk expanded in numbers, and by the 1930s they were common throughout the Rockies portion of the East Kootenay. Transplants from Yellowstone into Banff and Jasper National Parks helped the process. In the 1940s elk crossed the valley into the Purcells. By the 1950s there were elk everywhere. We have no real idea as to how many there were, but there were lots. Some estimates are as high at twenty thousand.

The early estimates were just guesses, but from the 1970s on, there were amazing elk numbers in the Palliser and Middle Fork country. It was classic backcountry hunting—people with horses, hunting in high basins and on lonely ridges, which was and still is the best damn hunting experience there is. As for folks who just like to look at elk, you could see the herds resting in high meadows throughout the Rockies. Throughout this time period, we had large numbers of elk that wintered in the lower valleys, especially in the Trench. And most of them migrated each spring into the high valleys of the Rockies and the Purcells. There they provided a living for a bunch of outfitter families like the Tegarts, Mitchells, Coopers, Christensens, Andersons, Dubois, Campsalls, Alfred Joseph and many others. It was a wonderful time if you loved wild country and especially if you loved wild country that was full of wildlife.

Two things were at play in earlier decades. Much of the East Kootenay Trench burned in the 1930s, creating large grassland and shrub land areas that were perfect winter range for elk and other ungulates. And predator numbers were very low. Wolves were very uncommon due to poisoning throughout the mountains, including the national parks, in response to a rabies scare in the 1940s. Grizzlies were around, but they were hunted over bait (dead horses) in those days, and there were nowhere near the numbers of bears around that there are today. Cougars were hunted by some locals and by the conservation officers and were very uncommon. Black bears were present and were hunted also, but they seemed fairly common when I first came into the country in the 1970s.

Two things have happened in more recent decades. Elk have stopped migrating into the mountains the way they used to, and overall elk numbers have declined substantially. Since we have minimal funding in this province for doing serious science-based wildlife management, we don't really know why this had happened. But we can guess, based on work done in other areas. Our best tool for understanding what is happening to elk populations is not estimates of actual numbers but estimates of something called calf recruitment. Elk herds need to have "recruitment," i.e., young calves coming into the population every year to replace the older cows and bulls that die. A herd needs twenty to thirty calves per one hundred cows surviving their first winter to go into the population. If the ratio is less than that, the herd will collapse; if it is higher, the herd will expand in numbers. In the 1970s and 1980s elk calf numbers were very high, from forty to sixty per one hundred cows. The elk herd could expand and could handle large human harvests of both bulls and cows. Then, about 1992, calf ratios dropped to twenty-five to thirty per one hundred, which is at the margin in terms of herd survival. Ratios have stayed in that range ever since, with a few years in the thirty-plus range. This decline in calf production coincided with the increase in all four large predators. The critical point is not that predators kill elk, but that they kill large numbers of calf elk. As a result, they seriously affect calf ratios, which in turn can have major impacts on elk populations over time.

Many biologists suggest that this decline is a result of loss of habitat. However, unlike many such biologists, I actually go out and take a look each spring at the grasslands on our various winter ranges. The grass is simply not being used by wildlife, or cattle, in most areas. The problem is something other than habitat.

Wolves first came into the East Kootenay in significant numbers in the last few decades. Cody saw some of the first to arrive. They are now common throughout the Kootenays and the mountain parks. Grizzly bear numbers have increased substantially from earlier times. There are now four thousand to five thousand grizzlies in the Canadian Rockies, the Kootenays and northern Montana. Black bear numbers are likely about twice that number. Cougar numbers are also high. We have gone from a situation where we had limited numbers of all four large predators to now, where we have high densities of all four species. It is not just the arrival of wolves that is of concern here. It is the combined impact of all four major predators that is affecting ungulate populations. There are now solid scientific studies that show that bears have a huge impact on calf ratios in elk and other ungulates.

A few years ago Shannon Barber-Meyer collared 142 calf elk in northern Yellowstone in early June when they were easy to catch. By December 100 of those calves were dead. Before winter. Of those that died, two died of disease and all the rest were killed by predators. About 75 were killed by bears. More recently a biologist in Alaska, Chris Brockman, put small cameras on the collars of eight grizzlies in country with lots of grizzlies, moose and caribou. These bears killed an average of 1.2 calves per day over the calves' first month of life, when they were relatively easy to catch. This amounts to 25 to 35 calves per bear for the spring period. In southern Montana, other researchers looked at elk calf recruitment and found that in that area, most of the calves were killed by cougars and not recently arrived wolves.

In my view, it is the impact of bears in early spring, followed by predation by other predators during the rest of the year, that has driven the decline in ungulates here. This is primarily by bears killing calves and reducing recruitment to levels that can't support the herds over time.

This had played out for Cody and the Palliser in the following ways. Elk often came into the Palliser from Banff National Park. The only elk left in the south portion of Banff National Park now are living in the town of Banff itself. They never go more than a few kilometres from town. In the past there were two large elk herds that wintered in the Beaverfoot Valley (north of Kootenay National Park) and in the Upper Kootenay Valley, primarily in the Salt Lake flats close to where the Palliser comes out of the mountains. There were something like three hundred to four hundred head in the Beaverfoot. They are all gone. The Upper Kootenay Valley herd that was three hundred to five hundred head in earlier years is now down to twenty or thirty head.

None of the outfitters in the area from the Beaverfoot to the Palliser have killed an elk in the last five years. The situation is very similar in the backcountry in the Purcell range. Almost no elk have been taken there also. The collapse of the backcountry elk populations that Cody watched in the Palliser is not a situation that has occurred just in the Palliser; it has occurred throughout most of the mountains of the East Kootenay. This has occurred along with a decline in overall numbers from fourteen thousand in 2009 to ten thousand in 2014 to seven thousand in 2018 in the Trench.

This is not a pretty picture for those of us who like a little wildlife with our mountains. Over this same time period, people from outside areas, primarily Vancouver, have fallen in love with predators based on stories told by environmental groups that are just plain wrong. So the grizzly bear hunting season is now closed across the province. And when the Wildlife Branch tried to reduce wolf numbers to save an endangered caribou population (in the West Kootenay), over one hundred thousand people signed a petition opposing the only management action that could save those little herds. I think we are headed for a time where wildlife and especially elk are no longer a part of the landscape or the culture of the East Kootenay. Uninformed people will tell you that if the ungulate numbers go down, then predator numbers will decline, and we will start a new cycle and ungulate numbers will increase again. There are some solid science-based reasons to suggest that this will not happen. The bottom line is that in Banff National Park, with no hunting, elk numbers have been down to a few hundred head for almost two decades. Despite massive increases in available habitat in the backcountry there as a result of controlled burns, the numbers have remained low.

We have traded healthy populations of elk, sheep, moose, mule deer, goat, some grizzlies, black bears, a few cougars and very few wolves, for a system with no elk, very few moose, almost no mule deer, some goats, a few bighorn sheep, and just enough whitetails to maintain a low-level population of cougars and wolves. Bears will decline less, since they are omnivores and are not directly dependent on meat. And no, it will not cycle back, not without management.

Is there a future for wildlife—that is, high numbers of all large mammals—in the Rockies and East Kootenays? Not in my view. That sad fact will be a direct result of the incorrect belief systems of the general public and an embarrassing number of wildlife ecologists, who are willing to ignore the facts and toe the politically correct nonsense that has created this situation.

It may well be that the times that were shared by Cody and Erwin and Garrett and Don and me, along with all the outfitters and guides in the East Kootenay region, will not be seen again. The mountains are still spectacular, the lakes lovely and blue, the forests dark and green, but it somehow will be different without wildlife. Young people who go to the mountains will, like us, get up in the middle of the night to have a pee and look at the stars on cold September nights, but unlike us, they will not have the wonderful serenade of bugling elk interrupting their late-night business.

THE TRAIL ENDS

BY ANDY

Something Cody and I both passionately agreed on was the damage done to our wild areas and the wildlife within by government bungling throughout the years. In our younger years we had enjoyed unprecedented opportunities to make a living in the mountains. In our opinion, the Social Credit governments under the Kelowna Bennett dynasty seemed to govern for the entire province. Sure, they may have been a little too industry friendly, but the province seemed to be awash in decent-paying jobs.

A lot of small communities throughout the province were built with forestry and mining. Both provided good, well-paying jobs that allowed their workers to buy homes and raise their families with a decent lifestyle. Cody worked as a logger for many years during the off-season, as the guiding business never made enough to see him through the year. While the government was business friendly, it was staffed by a decent contingent of foresters, biologists and conservation officers who were responsible for the stewardship of our precious resources. If you spent time in the bush, you would invariably run into those individuals who were actually out in the field enforcing that stewardship. This of course made industry more responsible, and while it was not perfect, the environment was somewhat protected. Tree-farm licences required that the logs be milled within a certain area, which resulted in thriving mill towns throughout the province.

Then a drastic change occurred in 1968. The power of premier moved to the coast and would never leave. The rapidly expanding Lower Mainland would exert its influence throughout the entire province, and politicians of all stripes would pander to the masses of urban dwellers rather than provide balance for the entire province. That brought on the demise of the once powerful Social Credit Party and with an NDP blip resulted in the pro-industry Liberal Party, which would govern for decades. They believed that industry should run unfettered, and they gutted those departments such as forestry and wildlife that had provided stewardship and enforcement for our precious wilderness areas. Allowing industry to monitor itself would prove disastrous for the wilderness and the small towns that relied on those industries.

In the forest industry, rules were relaxed, allowing massive clear-cuts to be the norm. Tree-farm licensing requirements were relaxed, allowing forest companies to move lumber processing farther afield, effectively killing the economic driver of many small communities.

Although Cody had parted company with his beloved Palliser territory, he kept his hand in the life by guiding hunts for other outfitters. He was particularly upset with the new NDP/Green coalition government's decision to end the grizzly hunt despite the Auditor General's report stating that the grizzly population was healthy and well managed. Aside from the lost revenue for guide outfitters throughout the province, he, like Bob Jamieson, understood that the decision wasn't just based on bad science, but on no science at all. He was right. The decision was simply politically expedient, with no regard to the people it would be hurting the most.

My personal take on the issue is that the government simply caved to a vocal lobby from the Fur-Bearers Association, West Coast environmental groups and other anti-hunting organizations who had mounted a sophisticated campaign of media manipulation designed to outrage urban dwellers. It started with the Great Bear Rainforest campaign, which resulted in that area being closed to hunting. It featured press releases and media interviews from their pet biologists claiming that the grizzly population was threatened, despite the government's own science saying otherwise. This was coupled with providing the media with cute videos of mama bears and cubs frolicking, compared with a video some unfortunate hunter posted on YouTube of a kill where the bear ended up falling down a slide after being shot, while the hunters cheered. The death of any animal is not a pretty sight, even with a perfect kill shot, so it becomes easier to manipulate the emotions of non-hunters by releasing something like this to the media.

Also, this group and others had worked hard at making "trophy hunter" a dirty term. Shame, how could you kill this beautiful animal just to mount its head on your wall or make a rug? They apply it with prejudice to anyone who hunts for a trophy elk, deer, goat, sheep or moose, even though BC has had a law on the books forever, requiring any hunter who harvests an animal to take and use the carcass, with the exception of grizzlies. The Fur-Bearers group commissioned Insights West for a series of polls starting in 2015. That province-wide poll of eight hundred misused the term "trophy hunter" to get its desired results. Of course, a majority of respondents were against it but were okay about hunting for meat. Again, this was sheer stupidity, because in almost all cases, the two are the same. Give me a steak from a trophy bull elk any day.

In later polls aimed directly at the grizzly hunt, 89 percent of responders were non-hunters, and some questions had as low as eighteen respondents. The polls also asked what political party respondents voted for. In my opinion this was political manipulation of the worst kind, resulting in decisions based on polls, which can easily be skewed, rather than on science. Other arguments were made based on the economic benefits of bear viewing rather than hunting. It was reported that bear viewing was a greater benefit economically to the province than grizzly hunting. A small group of bear-viewing businesses, which are primarily located in the Great Bear Rainforest, made the economic argument that bear viewing created more revenue than the grizzly hunt. They claimed the entire estimated revenue from ecotourism province-wide, which includes whale watching and multiple nature tours, and compared it against the revenue generated by the grizzly hunt alone. One such claim compared the bear-watching industry revenue against the hunt in that region only, as opposed to that of the whole province. As we all know, statistics can be manipulated to show whatever you want them to show.

So, what's going to happen now that grizzlies can no longer be hunted, except by First Nations hunters for ceremonial purposes? I believe Bob Jamieson is on the money with his prediction of a huge decline in the elk, deer and moose populations due to an unchecked grizzly population. As these apex predators totally lose their fear of man, there will be more disastrous interactions between bears and humans. This will intensify even more as the ungulate population fades and grizzlies search for new food supplies. There have been recent examples of this lately, with several grizzly attacks and a video shown on Global BC of a three-year-old grizzly chasing after a kayaker and almost catching him.

As for guide outfitters in British Columbia, unfortunately, I must agree with Bob Jamieson's assessment of their future challenges. The grizzly hunt provided an infusion of revenue needed for economic survival for some small operators. Now, the increased depredation of the ungulate population by increased numbers of grizzlies and wolves will impact the success rate of the fall hunt and put even more economic pressure on these mostly family-run businesses. Those of us who cherish the wild spaces and love the thrill of the hunt can only hope that in the near future we get a government in BC that shows real leadership for the entire province and follows the science rather than the polls.

For future generations, we can only hope they have the opportunity to ride the wild trails and experience the magic of nature away from social media, cellphones and the trappings of civilization. We can hope they get to experience the thrill of a bull elk bugling on a frosty morning and the excitement of the hunt, followed by the satisfied and tired feeling of sitting in a smoky cabin with a strong drink as they smell elk steaks cooking on the grill. We can hope they get to experience the majesty of a blue mountain lake and the thrill of dropping a fly in front of a ten-pound cutthroat. That was our reality.

While Cody's amazing journey, which started in 1950, came to an end in spring 2018, this also spells the end of our journey through the past, which started in the pub in Radium about four years ago. Although my journey with him started fifty years ago in high school, I also got to know the man that he had become, and over the intense past year of writing, I was able to fill in those lost years. I also came to realize how much that early friendship changed my entire life. Cody taught me so much about being fearless in those early years, and he constantly pushed me beyond my comfort level. Those lessons stuck with me throughout my life and I believe made me a better man. I recall one recent Christmas when Cody called while visiting his daughter Amber. He had enjoyed a few tots of rum, as had I, and we talked about the book and the past. As he went to hang up, he said, "I love you guys!"

I was going to reply with some smart remark, as in our younger days we were too tough to say stuff like that, but I didn't. I'm not sure what my reply actually was, but buddy, I love you too. You were a hell of a man and I hope your story did you proud. I'm going to let your brother Garrett have the last say.

A POEM FOR MY BROTHER

GARRETT TEGART

This poem I wrote for Cody
My brother, closest to my heart
Of course, it's all about the hunt
And a great place to start.

We've rode a lot of horses
Some, the quiet and solid steeds
Some of them were outlaws
Green broke and downright dirty mean.

We've had our share of wrecks
As we headed up the trail
Chasing a bull elk's bugle
On the wind, you heard him wail.

Old eagle-eye Cody
Would spot him on the run
His .30-06 would clear leather
My brother was having fun.

High up on a mountain
We caped that big bull out
Scored up his rack, he was a good one
Of that there was no doubt.

Quartered up, and diamond hitched
Near dark and losin' light
Hopin' the pack horse wouldn't buck him off
With the end of the hunt in sight.

Tomorrow is unwritten
But I'm sure we'll have a plan
Maybe we'll just go fishin'
Trout for the frying pan.

ACKNOWLEDGEMENTS

BY ANDY

First and foremost, to my good friend Hiram Cody Tegart, thanks for living a life full of adventures worth writing about.

On behalf of Cody and myself, thanks to all the guides and hunters who contributed their stories: Randy Atwood, Dr. Ervin Hess, Don Koopmans, Ervin Morneau, Garrett Tegart, Texas Tim and Gary Weatherby.

Also, a special thanks to Bob Jamieson for the stories he contributed and for sharing his substantial knowledge of the dire issues the ungulate population is facing in the Rocky Mountain Trench.

Thanks to Cody's brother Garrett, his sister Susan and his daughter Ashley for filling in some of the blanks, and to Louise Land and Sarah Maltby for helping Cody get his stories into type. Thanks to my good friend Maryon Fijnvandraat for her technical assistance.

Finally, thank you to my wife, Deena, for her patience during this, my labour of love.

PHOTO: ASHLEY TEGART

HIRAM CODY TEGART (Cody) was born in 1950 to a pioneering family in the Columbia Valley of British Columbia. He grew up on a ranch near Brisco where he learned to ride, shoot and work hard at a young age. Some of his earliest memories were of watching men ride off to his dad's hunting territory and wanting so badly to join them. He learned to pack a horse and throw a diamond hitch and spent many of his summers in the hills. After high school, Cody tried his hand at being a carpenter in Calgary but the mountains called him back. Eventually he purchased the guiding business from his father in 1979 and ran it successfully before selling it in 1993. He continued to guide for others and in the off-season he logged and ran heavy equipment. He retired in 2017 and moved to Winfield, Alberta. Cody passed away in the spring of 2018.

PHOTO: DEENA RICHARDS

ANDREW BRUCE RICHARDS was born in Hudson Bay, Saskatchewan, in 1953. He lived on a small farm there, then moved to Flin Flon, Manitoba, where he developed his love of the outdoors. At age thirteen he moved with his mother to the Columbia Valley in British Columbia. He met Hiram Cody Tegart (Cody) in high school, where they developed a close friendship that would last ten years and rekindle twenty years later. After guiding one season for Cody's father, Andy married his high school sweetheart and went to work in the forest industry. Deciding his future didn't lie there, he enrolled in the Journalism Arts Advertising Program at the Southern Alberta Institute of Technology. Starting in 1980, he worked at weekly newspapers in Quesnel, Salmon Arm and Victoria before joining the *Times Colonist Daily*. With small-town life calling, Andy and his wife moved to Summerland in 2001. After sixteen years with the *Penticton Herald,* he retired in 2016 and now spends his time doing the things he loves in the great outdoors.